THE VENDING PORTAL

THE VENDING PORTAL

JUDY LIU

To my sister Amber for always believing in me.

CONTENTS

PART ONE   **9**

PROLOGUE   11

CHAPTER 1   17

CHAPTER 2   25

CHAPTER 3   37

CHAPTER 4   55

CHAPTER 5   65

CHAPTER 6   69

CHAPTER 7   73

PART TWO   **89**

CHAPTER 8   91

CHAPTER 9   101

CHAPTER 10   109

CHAPTER 11   115

CHAPTER 12   135

CHAPTER 13   149

CHAPTER 14   157

CHAPTER 15   167

CHAPTER 16   177

PART THREE   **191**

CHAPTER 17   193

CHAPTER 18   205

CHAPTER 19   219

CHAPTER 20   229

CHAPTER 21   239

EPILOGUE   247

ACKNOWLEDGMENTS   249

PART ONE

PROLOGUE

Clouds rolled in as the sky dimmed with the onset of night. The sun hadn't quite gone down, setting a gray, purplish filter across the landscape and distant mountains. The town itself was quiet. Most residents were already inside cooking and eating dinner, and the lights from within homes shined through the wooden slats of the windows. At the far side of the street, a man emerged out of darkness, taking quick, purposeful strides as his trench coat flapped in the wind. His hat teetered on his head and made to fly off when his left arm whipped out of his pocket to keep it in place, just in time. With one hand still holding down his hat, the man seemed to be in a hurry and would occasionally glance around. No one was in sight— just the glowing lights from dining families inside houses and closed storefronts lining the narrow street.

A zap sounded in the distance. The man paused mid-step, glanced over his shoulder hastily, and made the next right turn into a narrower alley. His pace quickened as he made his way through the backstreet, every so often contorting his body to slip between the buildings. After a few blocks, he made it to the outskirts of town, which marked the start of rice paddies that went on as far as the eye could see. The man furtively looked around, checked the watch on his wrist, and continued his trek down the road between the fields.

"You'd think we could rendezvous at a closer location," the man muttered under his breath. Rain began falling lightly, and a streak of lightning cut across the sky in the distance. The road between the fields was raised above them, and the fields were like large, square holes on either side of the road to allow for flooding for the crop. Just ahead stood a small shack on the roadside. He had to get there. He walked faster when he heard another zap, only this time, it came from in front of him, right where the shack was.

"Just on time," he growled as he took up a light jog toward the shack. As he approached, a woman in a tight bun and long trench coat emerged from within.

"Hey, Howler. Took you long enough," she greeted the man as he slowed to a stop in front of her.

"I had to get some enforcers off my trail, Romilda. Cut me some slack. I still think someone followed me, so we have to be quick. Did you bring it?" the man named Howler responded. As another streak of lightning broke across the sky, the split second of light showed Romilda's pale face and an emblem with elephant tusks on the shoulders of both their trench coats.

"Yes, it wasn't easy to lug over here. No one's ever transported a portal device through another. Not sure if it messed with the mechanics, but it should still work and get us home." Romilda groaned as she put a hand on the vending machine next to her for support. "We just have to power it up, but it should blend in and be safe here," Romilda continued as she took a large gulp out of a bottled drink in her hand labeled *Mensen*.

The vending machine of snacks she was leaning against stood next to another already plugged into the outside wall of the shack. That one was a beverage machine. However, it didn't have the drink labeled *Mensen* in its bright display of drinks. Romilda had brought her drink from someplace else.

"Why is there even a shack here?" Howler mused out loud, forgetting his earlier rush. As the engineer, he was always eager to understand how everything works and sometimes got distracted by questions that spontaneously popped into his mind "What's this structure for?"

Romilda shrugged as she finished downing her drink. "While I was waiting for you inside, I saw some boots and farming tools." She already sounded better than earlier after taking the drink. "It's probably a place for the rice farmers to store the tools they need. I don't see any houses nearby, so they probably live far from here."

"Hmm, I guess it's not very convenient to transport everything to the fields every time," Howler ruminated. "I just thought it strange at first that this is here and there's a vending machine. But I suppose even farmers need a drink during hot, tiring days."

"Let's get to it. You have the stone?" Romilda was ready to address the task at hand now that she'd finished her drink and color returned to her face. "You know we couldn't have the stone and machine together while we were followed. We can't lose both if one of us were captured."

"Yes, I have it." Howler took off his hat, reached into a sewn pocket on the inside, and pulled out a glowing blue stone.

ZAP, ZAP. They heard two zaps in the distance toward the town from which Howler came, and both immediately tensed.

"Hurry, the enforcers are closer than expected. We can't let them know we brought a machine to this place. The one we have is unregistered," Romilda's voice suddenly dropped to a low whisper and wasn't as carefree as before.

"We also went through the trouble of changing out the insides to hold snacks instead of beverages as a disguise," Howler added.

"Right. It'd ruin our entire mission if they see through the disguise and discover its existence. Now, let's get it working and get out!"

"It takes time to power up!" Howler whispered back as he kneeled and felt around the machine. He opened something at the bottom corner of the back of the machine and slipped his hand in to place the stone. They could hear the machine starting to whirr, but the lights within its display were not lighting up yet. Romilda glanced in the distance and back at the machine. She was starting to hear the footsteps of someone running toward them.

"I think they're here! Come on! This way!" a voice called as the rain started to fall harder. At this point, the machine still was not lighting up.

Romilda was getting anxious and shaking her right leg as she stood. "It wasn't supposed to be this close, Howler. What's wrong with the machine? Or is the stone faulty?"

Howler felt around the back of the machine, trying to figure out the issue. "I don't know... sure it takes time, but not this long. And I'm confident the stone is fine."

The sound of running steps in gathering puddles was getting louder.

Romilda knew it'd be too close. She had to draw them away. She couldn't let them even suspect they could have brought a machine here even if they'd already disguised it. Although she needed the machine to get home, as the team leader, she was ready to draw the enforcers away from Howler so he could troubleshoot how to get the machine working and go home. She could always come back later after she shook off the enforcers, but she didn't have the engineering knowledge Howler had to ensure the machine was functioning.

She stopped shaking her legs in anxiousness and stood firm. "Howler, I will draw them away. You keep working on the machine and then you leave."

Howler stopped what he was doing and looked at her. "This wasn't the plan. We are not to split up."

"Plans change," Romilda responded as she reached into her trench coat for some handheld devices and tapped a screen on a bracelet, "I'm ordering you to do as you're told. Get the machine working. Stay hidden. Go home. I'll follow soon after." Before Howler could get another word in, Romilda stepped out from behind the shack and started running farther down the road, away from the coming footsteps.

"I hear someone ahead!" a rough voice called out.

Farther down the road, Howler saw a flash of light revealing the outline of Romilda in the distance, mid-stride as she ran. *Clever lady, she must have used a blinder device to distract the enforcers in the dark and draw them past the shed,* Howler thought quickly in awe.

"Over there! They're over there!"

Howler sensed they were close, so he slipped down the slope of the road, away from the shack, and into one of the muddy rice paddies lining the road, hoping the enforcers wouldn't see him.

Two figures ran by right as he slipped into the paddy. In the waning light of the sky, Howler spotted the burgundy-purple suits, glints of gold buttons and embroidery, and outlines of bucket hats as they whizzed by and paid no attention to the shack. He breathed a sigh of relief and silently hoped Romilda would be okay. He sloshed around a bit in the mud, apologetic for ruining some of the sprouting rice stalks, and started climbing back up the slope to the road and shack.

Wait, why did I only see two enforcers? Howler paused. He put up his fingers to count. *I'm pretty sure I heard three zaps in total, one in the town and two later...* Hoping to get a better look in the dark at the road, Howler got up from his crouch, but as he straightened his legs to stand so his head would be level with the raised road, a head donned with a burgundy bucket hat was staring right at Howler. The third enforcer had been kneeling at the edge of the road. Howler couldn't see him from below in the paddy. In horror, Howler took a step back and tripped as his boot got caught in the mud.

"Gotcha." The enforcer smiled while shining a flashlight in Howler's face.

Howler glanced at the shack next to the third enforcer, who was now making his way down to him. To his relief, the snack machine's display light was now on and didn't look a hair out of place. He closed his eyes. His mission was complete.

CHAPTER 1

Mel watched the clock at the corner of the classroom, twirling her pencil as the teacher droned on about world history. Today, they were learning about the Bronze Age and the replacement of stone tools with metals. She'd already finished the class worksheet and was waiting for the clock to hit 2:30 p.m. Every Tuesday, she volunteered at the local animal shelter, where she could help them with paperwork or feeding time or play with the animals to keep them company. It was a time Mel looked forward to every week.

Becca, Mel's best friend, tossed a neatly folded piece of paper onto her desk. Mel opened it.

Hang out after school today? My house? My mom said you could stay for dinner.

The paper was replete with cute doodles Beck made during class.

Mel flipped the note over and scrawled on the back.

Can't today, sorry! I volunteer every Tuesday, remember? And my sister doesn't have after-school club today, so I need to walk her back home. Come to my place tomorrow?

She carefully folded it and tossed it back onto Beck's desk. Beck opened it, and her eyes scanned the note. She turned to Mel, made a pout, and then a beaming thumbs up, agreeing to hang out tomorrow. Mel gave a thankful grin.

The final school bell dinged, and students immediately stood up and started packing their stationery and notebooks, including Mel and Beck.

"Remember to read chapter eleven and complete the handout you will pick up at the door! The Bronze Age is exciting!" the teacher called out above the sounds of rustling papers and shuffling chairs. Mel finished stuffing her books into her book bag when Beck approached, setting a handout on her desk.

"Thanks, Beck." Mel placed the handout inside a folder. "Sorry, I can't hang out today. But come over tomorrow. I'll tell my mom."

"Yeah, I'll stop by tomorrow! I completely forgot you volunteer today. Can't keep the days of the week straight here." Beck tapped her head with a laugh. They both slung their book bags across their shoulders and headed out together. They chattered about the latest shows they watched, what high schools they were hoping to get into, the homework assignments they had for the day, and how Beck was at her wit's end with her baby brother.

"He just... cries all the time! All night!"

"Well, what do you expect, Beck? He's a baby," Mel laughed, though she sympathized.

Beck frowned playfully. "My parents say it'll get better as he gets older. I sure hope so!" She looked toward the school's front gates as they'd crossed the courtyard and neared it to exit the school. "Oh, hey, Sage!" She waved at Mel's little sister, who was in fourth grade, three years younger than Mel and Becca.

"Hey, Becca. Hey, Mel," Sage responded morosely.

"No basketball practice today?" Becca asked Sage as the three of them fell into line, walking side by side.

"Not today. I think Coach is focusing on track practices for their track meet next week," Sage said. Mel thought she looked a little down. She knew Sage treated practices like hang outs with her friends, and she didn't like being left out of gatherings or events.

"I'm this way." Beck interrupted Mel's thoughts as she pointed down an intersection to their left. "See you all tomorrow!" She skipped off in the direction she pointed.

"So, did anything fun happen at school today?" Mel asked Sage.

"Not really. Most people I know are also on the track team, so they're all together right now and talking about that." The majority of Sage's friends on the Northridge Elementary team were on both the track and basketball teams. As such, Sage begged to be on both to be with them, but their parents had mandated Sage choose one as they worried she wouldn't have enough time for home-work or other activities. "They're probably all having fun or talking, and I'm not there. What if there's some new inside joke that I miss?"

"With a track meet coming up, hopefully, they're just focused on training?" Mel tried unsuccessfully to comfort her. She didn't know what else to talk about to cheer Sage up as they walked for a bit in silence, but then an idea popped into her head.

"Hey. What do you say we take another route home?" she enticingly said to Sage.

Sage looked up from the ground as they were walking and at Mel. "Where?"

Mel thought for a moment. "Well, there are those fields Mom and Dad sometimes drive past when we go on road trips to visit family. We've never gotten to explore there. Plus, the rice fields should be filled with tall stalks now. It'll be pretty!"

Sage's small, round face lit up. Mel knew Sage didn't want to go home just yet and what she needed was a distraction from the fact that she was not with the rest of her friends. Sage had always liked to explore, and usually, it was Sage pulling Mel around to check out new things.

They walked past the turn to their neighborhood and continued down the main street. Mel remembered the street to the fields included an older section of town that served as a tourist attraction now, but she'd always liked the shops there. Residents called it Old Town. *Sage will love that, and we haven't checked that out in a while.* As they walked, smells of street food wafted into their nostrils. They'd reached the Old Town section, and it was bustling. Stores lining the street had their doors slid open, welcoming visitors and shoppers. Street vendors were at the edges of the street outside the stores, cooking up a storm on their carts. People were walking around with beautifully packaged bags of purchased goods in their hands. Mel looked down at Sage and saw her beaming. It seemed Sage had forgotten she wasn't hanging out with her friends while they were all together.

"Let's go to that sweets shop!" Sage pointed at the second shop to their right.

"That's a great idea," Mel agreed. These shops usually handed out samples, and there were many other children inside, trying to get their fill without letting their parents know before they got home. After Mel and Sage had tasted all the sweets they could, they explored the other shops. One was selling ice cream sandwiches on rice crackers, another specialized in wind chimes, and another advertised gold leaf on all sorts of items like bowls, plates, skin care, cookies, you name it.

The two of them were happily snacking on a shared ice cream rice cracker sandwich when they reached the edge of the Old Town. The strip wasn't very long. Mel was sure that Old Town used to be larger, but that strip was the only preserved section. The rest likely was pulled down to erect more modern buildings, including the Northridge schools they attend.

Mel and Sage were greeted with a sea of green stalks, waving in the wind and lining the road. It was idyllic walking among the rice stalks with the mountains in the distance. There weren't many people around this road, mostly used for long-distance driving to other towns and cities. They'd occasionally see a car pass as they walked. Sage, now in better spirits, was prattling away about school, her friends, and new plays they tried in basketball, when she suddenly stopped.

"Mel, look!" She pointed at a small structure in the distance on the side of the road, next to the fields. "Let's check that out!" She started running over.

"Sage, wait!" Mel sprinted after her. Sage was always running off, and at this point, Mel thought that she really should be used to it. Fortunately, Mel was taller and faster than Sage and was able to catch up even though Sage got a head start.

"Is this a bus stop?" Sage looked at the structure as they got to it. Mel saw the pole with a bus stop number in front of the structure. It was an open steel frame with a flat roof and a bench underneath for people to sit or stay out of the rain if the weather was bad.

"Yeah, I think so. Who knew there could be a bus stop out here?" Mel looked back at where they came from and hadn't realized they'd walked so far from Old Town. She could still see it, but it was much smaller in the distance, and they could no longer hear the calls of employees from shops to entice people in or the chattering of those walking the streets.

Sage had walked to the farther end of the bus stop shelter and peeked behind the wall. "There are vending machines here! Do you think it's for people if they get hungry or thirsty while they wait?"

Mel walked over to Sage, and sure enough, two vending machines were lining the outside wall of the bus stop shelter, facing away from where they came from so they wouldn't have seen it if they didn't walk farther. "Yeah, that's neat. Buses probably don't stop at this bus stop very often, so they have some snacks if you get hungry as you wait." In fact, Mel was starting to feel a bit hungry as a shared ice cream sandwich earlier wasn't enough, and she took a step closer to examine the options. The beverage machine was on and working but a bit battered from being out in the elements. The snack machine, on the other hand, was in a different state. The lights in the display were off, and the clear plastic sheet to see through the snacks display was a bit clouded. Some jasmine flower bushes were growing next to the snack machine, with their branches partially covering some of the display. *Ugh,*

I wanted food, not drinks, but the snack machine seems out of commission.

Sage looked at the machine from around Mel's back. "Looks really old and broken—kind of cool. I've never seen these snacks around," she pointed out.

Mel was so busy pressing random buttons, wondering if any would elicit a reaction from the dead machine, that she didn't look carefully at the display of snacks. She paused and brought her face closer. She saw a snack package advertising a purple-looking crescent cracker, cylindrical packages picturing pebble-like snacks, and candy bars she'd never seen.

"How strange. You're right. What are these?"

Sage shrugged. "Maybe old snacks from Mom's and Dad's time?" Then her eyes lit up. "What if we could get one of these to bring back to Mom and Dad? They'd love it if it's from their time!"

Mel laughed. "That's a good idea if they actually recognize these. This is a great find! But the machine's broken."

"Yeah, but I'm sure if I just reach in from the bottom, I can get one." Sage knelt down, stuck her right arm through the bottom, where one usually grabs the purchased item, and started reaching upward. Mel could see Sage's hand peek out at the bottom of the display. She pressed herself against the display in excitement.

"Wait, I think you *could* reach one! Just a little farther! If you can grab the corner of a bag, maybe you can pull it down."

Sage's face was contorted in concentration while she tried to twist her arm and push it in more. She was just a smidgen away from pinching the corner of the package with the purple crackers to pull it down. "I... can't... get it.

Ugh!" Sage pulled her arm out in frustration and stood up. They both stared at the snack bag they almost got.

"I think if we shake it to get it to move down a bit more, I can reach it," Sage mused. Mel tried to shake the machine, but it wouldn't budge. She knocked on the machine's plastic sheet, but nothing moved.

"How about this?" Sage lifted her right foot backward, tried to align it to the row the snack bag was on, and swung her foot forward to kick it.

Mel suddenly felt the floor fall out from beneath her and her stomach lurched. Before she knew it, she felt she was being compressed, the breath squeezed out of her.

I... can't breathe.

Opening her mouth to gasp for air that was not there, she felt her lungs starting to burn and her head pounding in panic. Her vision blurred as her body twisted as if she had no bones. And as suddenly as it happened, she took in a big gulp of air and hit the ground.

CHAPTER 2

Mel immediately propped herself up with her arms, checking her extremities for any broken limbs, and coughed a few times, frazzled by the lack of air earlier. She seemed fine, but she found herself in front of the water fountains and restrooms of a park she'd never seen. It was a sunny day, and she could hear waves crashing on the shore nearby. *Where am I?*

But before Mel could take in more, she suddenly remembered. "Sage! Sage, where are you? Sage!"

"I'm here," Sage groaned from a few feet away. Mel shuffled over to her on her knees, "Hey, you okay?"

"Yeah, I think I'm good. But, what was *that*?" Mel knew what Sage was referring to. That feeling of suffocation.

"I don't know, but it looks like we're not around home." Mel took in her surroundings while helping Sage up. "I've never seen this park." Mel instantly felt quite queasy upon standing. Sage's lips, too, were looking a bit pale. Mel noticed a vending machine behind them, next to the water fountains. "Sage, let's grab some water or something from that vending machine. I'm feeling a bit dizzy."

Sage nodded silently, stopped, and ran into the restroom to throw up. While Mel heard her retching from outside the restroom, she staggered toward the vending machine. *Oh, nice... it's free.* There was no coin slot or credit card scanner on it. Instead, there was a small, bronze plaque with a message.

FOOD AND DRINK, COURTESY OF OUR PRIME MINISTER

Mel didn't dwell on that and looked through the selection. All of the beverages had the face of a young man plastered on them. *Is this a celebrity?* Then she noticed the one drink that didn't have this man's face printed on it. Instead, it had a large blue label with bold capital text: MENSEN. It was an unfamiliar brand, but she instinctively selected it so she wouldn't have to stare at a stranger's face in her hands. The vending machine started whirring, and the drink was pushed forward from the back, falling into the machine abyss. She reached in, grabbed the drink, and took a sip. To her surprise, it was a fizzy, slightly sweet drink, and although not what she expected, it seemed to clear the haze from her mind. *Ah, much better.* She felt a bump in her back pocket and remembered she had her cellphone. With relief, she took it out and flipped it open. *Hopefully, we can call someone, or I can pull up a map.* But to her dismay, her phone's screen remained dark and unresponsive.

Sage stumbled out of the restroom with a bit more color to her cheeks. "Oh, good. I need some of that," Sage said as she held her hand out for the drink. Mel handed it over, and Sage took a large gulp.

"Ah, now that's refreshing." Sage smacked her lips. "Now, where are we again?" Both Mel and Sage took a good look around.

"I'm not sure. Honestly," Mel took a sniff, "it smells like the jasmine flowers we just saw next to that vending machine by the rice paddies." Her eyes scanned around for the same flowers but didn't see them. Instead, her eyes were drawn to a yellow poster on the wall outside the restroom.

"Memory fades, but Reminserum is forever," Mel read aloud slowly, puzzled. "Hey, Sage, what do you suppose this means?" However, Sage wasn't next to her anymore either. Sage had walked away from the building on the path toward the park filled with young families. "Sage!" Mel forgot about the poster and ran to catch up. Slowing to a walk when she was next to Sage, Mel whispered, "What are you doing? Where are you going?"

"Nowhere," Sage responded. "I figured if we don't know where we are, let's look around." Mel rolled her eyes. She was always watching Sage, telling her to hang back or be quiet, but Sage seldom listened. Their whole family had constantly chided Sage to be less carefree and to think before speaking or acting lest she said something she shouldn't or put herself in an unsavory situation.

They walked side by side, with their bottled drink at hand, and tried to look at ease—as if they were taking a simple stroll through the park rather than trying to gather their bearings. A few parents were out with their young children and toddlers, and some eyed them warily as Mel heard what sounded like a school bell ring in the distance. *So, they have a school nearby... and I guess it is school hours right now.*

She turned to Sage. "Maybe we should get out of here soon. I think we're supposed to be in school or something. People are staring."

Sage nodded silently in response. She noticed too. They stopped proceeding down the path through the park and turned back toward the restrooms and vending machine. At least there, they could hide a bit in the shadows of the overhang of the building.

When they returned to where they initially found themselves, they took a seat on a bench and glanced around nervously.

"Now what?" Sage asked.

"I don't know. How do we get back?" They sat there for a few moments before Sage threw her hands up exasperatedly.

"Well, we definitely *can't* get back by just sitting here!" She got up and started examining the ground and area, looking carefully at the sidewalk cracks and vending machine slots. "Maybe there's a trigger somewhere. We were right at this spot, so maybe if we press something, it'll bring us back."

"Can you stop *doing* things? Stop doing whatever you want and touching stuff! Let's think about it first," Mel raised her voice in frustration.

Sage stopped and glared at Mel, "*You* stop telling me what to do! You and Mom and Dad and everyone! Nothing's going to happen if you just sit there silently!"

Mel had just about had it at this point. "You doing random things with that old vending machine at the fields is why we're here in the first place!" Her head was bursting. She couldn't deal with trying to figure out what was happening on top of trying to make sure Sage stayed out of trouble.

"You think it's *my* fault we're here?" Sage huffed. "We don't even know what happened!"

Mel resisted getting up from the bench in vexation. As the older sibling, she always thought it her duty to be above it and be more mature. She took several deep breaths, and that's when she noticed the familiar scent again. *It's the jasmine flowers we saw next to the old vending machine in the field earlier, but there are none here. Maybe Sage is onto something… If we can still smell the same flowers, perhaps we're just a button away from home.* She shook her head. *No way, that's bizarre. How could we still smell the same thing here? There's probably something else that smells similar at this park. That would make more sense.* As Mel pondered and Sage searched the area meticulously (yet fruitlessly in Mel's mind), a lady and her toddler walked over to the restrooms. Mel dipped her head, hoping her curtain of hair would hide her face. Sage paid no attention.

"Mom, what's this girl doing?" The child pointed at Sage as he teetered on his feet. Mel took a furtive glance and saw Sage still on the ground but sniffing a rock for some reason. The mom tried to block Sage from the child's line of sight by getting between them, "Don't pay that girl any mind. Bad kids skip school." She ushered her child toward the restroom.

"Mom, remember we have a play date set for later today, and I have a doctor's appointment scheduled for tomorrow morning at 8 a.m.," the child chimed.

"Oh, yes, thank you, Albo."

"And remember that other mother who just approached us? Her name is Tinabi. You met her last week at pottery class, and we now have a play date set with her child two weeks from now."

"Oh, right! Thank you for the name reminder. I may need you to remind me about the play date again in a few days."

"No problem, Mom." They kept chatting as they pushed through the restroom doors. "Remember also, Mom! This weekend, we—" The door swung shut.

How strange, Mel thought. *That little child sounds so much older than he looks. I've never heard any child speak to their mom like that. If anything, it should be the other way around! Maybe the child is just super smart?* She tried to rationalize her observation.

Before Mel could think much of it, a father with his son in his arms came to the vending machine. The man eyed Sage cautiously before switching his glance to Mel on the bench. He turned to his son in his arms, "All right, what do you want to drink? There's cider, apple juice, fig juice, vegetable juice, Mensen, and coffee, but that's for adults."

The child put his hand to his chin with a pensive expression before responding. "Mensen! I'm feeling a bit dizzy from all the running around I did, and I need to feel better for when we see Auntie and Uncle later today to be on good behavior."

The father's eyes widened. "I'd forgotten we're seeing them! Good thought, son!" He tousled the top of the child's head playfully, and the boy giggled. "One Mensen coming right up." The father clicked on a button on the vending machine, and the cloudy, translucent drink Mel and Sage had gotten earlier dropped to the bottom of the machine from the display. As the father handed the drink to his child and walked away, he took one quick backward glance at Mel and Sage again while addressing his son. "Yes, you must be on your best behavior today. You know Auntie McMannan is a stickler since she's an enforcer." He gave out a hearty laugh that sounded a bit forced to Mel.

"Yes, and remember Auntie McMannan doesn't like talking about her daughter because she's dating someone they don't approve of, so try not to bring up Cousin Tanya during dinner with them today," the child chirped didactically.

"Ah, right. Thank you. It would be bad if we brought that up. I'll remind your mother, too," the father responded as they walked away.

Okay, that's just bizarre. Mel thought the way the child talked was unsettling. *It's not just that first child. It's this little boy, too! They sound... almost like adults...*

After they were out of earshot, Mel loudly whispered to Sage, "Are you done yet? I do think we need to get out of here."

"I don't see you trying anything to help!" she snapped back petulantly.

Mel put a hand to her face. "Okay, true, but I don't think there's anything here. Let's at least move locations?"

Sage walked back to the bench from feeling up the bricks of the restroom building. "I guess I couldn't find anything other than that weird poster about memories, but did you hear that small kid? He sounded so strange. Kids we know don't speak like that."

"I was just thinking the same thing! Everything looks normal here, but it's all kind of different. It makes me uncomfortable. I *really* think we need to get out of here."

"Sure, I agree. But what's the rush? It's not like anyone's coming after u—"

"Over there, sir." They hear a deep voice in the distance. Mel turned toward the voice and saw the father from earlier pointing in their direction while speaking to a man in a burgundy-purple uniform lined with silver embroidery. He wore a matching bucket hat to complete the look. *A strangely dressed police officer?* The uniformed man looked over and started striding toward Mel and Sage.

"We've got to get out of here!" Sage whispered, her earlier tone transformed to panic. She was fidgeting, and Mel could almost envision Sage's eyes swiveling around her head, scanning the park for an escape.

"Stop! Don't make it too obvious!" Mel hurriedly whispered out of the corner of her mouth. To Mel, the uniformed man seemed to have a kind smile, and his gait wasn't rushed either. "If you look scared or run, then it's obvious we're not supposed to be here!" The man was getting within earshot, and while Mel was frantically whispering for Sage to calm down, Mel, too, was trying to find an escape. *It's all open space here. Running into the restroom would trap us. Running, in general, would result in a chase.* She took a sideward glance at the officer approaching. *No way we can outrun that. Dad beats us all the time in field games.* Heart racing, Mel decided the next best solution was to try talking their way out of this, and she held an ironclad grip on Sage's wrist to prevent her from bolting.

"Hey, kids." The officer was standing right next to them and kneeled with one knee to get to their eye level. "What're you both doing at the park? You know you should be in school, right?"

Mel forced her eyes to meet the officer's. Her voice felt stuck in her throat as she opened her mouth, and nothing came out. The officer waited patiently, but upon hearing nothing, he looked around, "Where are your parents? Which school do you go to?"

"We go to Northridge," Mel heard Sage squeak out the name of their school, and her stomach dropped when her sister said something without thinking. The officer raised a brow. "I'm not aware of any school by that name here. How far are you from home? And do your parents know you're here?" Mel's heart sank at the officer's comment that he'd never heard of their school. *Where could we be?* Upon receiving some blank stares, the officer sighed. "I'll need you both to come with me to the station. Then we'll call your parents and look up your school."

Wait. Wait! We can't run if we're at a police station. He doesn't even look like a police officer! Who is he? Mel screamed in her head. The hand she used to hold onto Sage started sweating profusely. The officer reached over to grab Mel's arm. *This is it. I don't know where we are. Mom and Dad will be so angry. Where am I? Who are these people?* Mel shut her eyes tightly while holding onto a quivering Sage.

"Excuse me, sir!" A boy about the same height as Mel had approached from behind the restroom building while the officer was addressing them. The man's gloved hand stopped midway as he looked toward the boy.

"Ah, Lewis. Shouldn't you be in school?"

"I am! We're on a field trip, and I think my classmates got lost, so I'm here to fetch them," the boy responded confidently. He made quick eye contact with Mel before looking away.

The officer looked questioningly at Sage, Mel, and then the boy named Lewis.

"Oh, yes, it's a multiple grade-level outing. We're on separate trips but in the same place." Lewis noticed it must have looked funny to have what looked like different-aged students on a field trip together. "I think the school does it from time to time if we're short on chaperones," he added and threw a glance at Mel as if asking her to play along. She was terrified, though, and her mouth felt sealed shut.

The officer looked at Lewis for a long while before he shrugged and sighed. "All right, Lewis. Don't be getting into trouble, all right? Tell your mom I said hello." He stood up, tipped his bucket hat with one hand, and walked away.

"Will do, sir!" Lewis called out and waved. He then looked at Mel and Sage. "I've been looking for you both everywhere!" he announced loudly.

"What're you—?" Sage started, but Mel caught on and immediately interrupted, "Sorry, we got lost. Thanks, Lewis." She glanced back at the officer walking away. She was typically good at listening and picking up details, so she remembered the boy's name when the officer addressed him.

"I'll take you both back. The group isn't far." Lewis started walking toward the side and around the back of the restroom building. He looked back. "Well, come on you two." He beckoned.

Mel and Sage exchanged glances, then looked back to the officer who now stood at a distance watching them. "Uh, yeah, we're coming!" They quickly got off the bench and followed Lewis.

As they followed Lewis, Mel couldn't help but examine him. After all, it wasn't difficult to stare at someone from behind. Lewis was about her height, with neatly combed side-parted, brown hair. He wore khaki shorts, dress shoes, long socks, and a navy suit jacket. *Looks like a school uniform.* He had the gait of someone who knew where he was going and occasionally whistled a few notes nonchalantly. They'd followed Lewis for several blocks, always about five feet behind. Mel had no idea where this strange boy was taking them, but she didn't dare say anything lest they anger him and he would leave them. However, at this moment, when Mel was pondering where they were going, Sage spoke up.

"Hey. Where are you taking us?" They were finally far enough from the bucket hat officer to speak freely.

Lewis stopped and turned around. "You know, a 'thanks' would be nice, seeing as I stopped you both from being taken by an enforcer."

CHAPTER 3

Lewis looked at them expectantly after reminding them he'd stopped the enforcer from taking them.

"Yeah, okay. Thank you for saving us from whatever that is," Sage ungraciously snapped before Mel could give a proper adage of gratitude. *But also, what's an enforcer?* Mel wondered.

"Now, where are you taking us again?" Sage continued.

"You don't have to follow me," Lewis responded very matter-of-factly. "If you have somewhere to be, then please go ahead." He gestured outward. Mel and Sage looked at each other.

"Give us a moment," Sage said. They turned their backs to Lewis and started whispering between the two of them.

"I don't know about him—seems fishy. He's a stranger!" Sage started.

"He has a point, though! We have nowhere to go. Where are we even? How do we get back?" Mel pointed out. "Also, what's an enforcer? That officer had a weird, purple uniform. I think we can learn more from this boy."

Sage ignored Mel's last comment. "Maybe we can go back to the restrooms and park and look around."

"And get questioned by an officer or... enforcer or whatever that man was?" Mel retorted. She saw fear flash behind Sage's eyes, and the stern expression left her face. They both glanced back at Lewis and gave a smile.

"Fine. He seems okay for now. But we need to be ready to run if things get dicey," Sage acquiesced.

Mel turned to face Lewis. "I think we got off on the wrong foot. My sister and I are grateful you helped earlier. Thank you for that. We overheard your name from that officer man, so we wanted to properly introduce ourselves. This is my sister, Sage," Mel placed a hand on Sage's arm, "and I'm Mel. We go to Northridge Elementary and Middle School. Can you help us get back?"

Lewis furrowed his brows. "I've never heard of those schools. Are you sure you have the name right?"

"Of course, we do. We've been going there for years," Sage snapped. Mel shot her a dirty look, and Sage huffed and turned away.

"Okay, okay." Lewis held both his hands out, seemingly surrendering. "Maybe my mom will know. There are many schools in the area, and I wouldn't know all of them. My house is just a few blocks away." And he set out at a leisurely stroll.

"Sometimes, when I don't feel like it, I'll skip school. But I'll still wear my school uniform in case I get stopped. I can just say I'm running an errand for school. It's nice to have some people who are also skipping school to walk with." Lewis tried to chat casually before the three of them fell into an awkward silence as they walked. Sage intermittently gestured wildly and mouthed messages to Mel behind Lewis's back, while Mel would respond back with softer gestures and expressions of puzzlement because she felt Sage was just being dramatic with her distrust of Lewis.

Mel noticed the sounds of crashing waves she'd heard earlier at the park were getting louder as they got closer to Lewis's house. As they walked, with Lewis slightly in front of Mel, and Sage warily walking behind Mel, Mel saw an opportunity to ask Lewis questions while they were still with him to learn more.

"So, you mentioned the uniformed man was an 'enforcer?'"

Lewis nodded. "Yup, he's the enforcer of this area. He's pretty nice and responds to anyone's complaints efficiently and quickly. He knows my mom because they went to the same school long ago, and they sometimes see each other at city council and government events, so I've known him since I was an infant. He keeps the neighborhood safe for us. Not all enforcers are like Enforcer Jovanna, though. Some sectors never get to interact with the enforcer who's leading their community protection. Today, someone probably spotted you two wandering alone and called Enforcer Jovanna. He was just concerned you were lost, so don't be too scared of him."

Mel thought about it. From how Lewis described it, it seemed like an enforcer was like a police officer, but with an emphasis on community support and mediation. "Do enforcers like Enforcer Jovanna also handle crimes?" Mel asked.

"Like home burglaries? Sure, Enforcer Jovanna looks into it with his team. He's good about getting involved, but not all of them do that. Some enforcers specialize in more heinous crimes, but my mom says we don't deal with too much of that anymore. Enforcers help us solve problems, check out neighbors' concerns, or they come to help someone, like get people's cats out of trees. Don't you have enforcers in your sector?"

"Oh, yes." Mel's mind was whirring to make an excuse for all her questions that probably sounded strange to anyone living in this place. She wasn't sure if they could trust this boy yet. It seemed this place was not Northridge or even another city. "Just... like you said, not every sector has an enforcer like Enforcer Jovanna, so it was a surprise seeing him and hearing how... involved he is. I was just curious if he does other things too in his job," Mel made up as she tried to maintain a steady voice.

"I see," Lewis responded. "I guess not every sector is like ours." He shrugged. "And, we're here! This is my house." With all this new information, while trying not to make it obvious to Lewis they weren't from around here, Mel hadn't noticed they'd reached a coastline and were walking along a cliffside that dipped into the ocean. They'd arrived at a two-story house at the edge of the cliff. It had wood paneling, painted a light periwinkle blue. Behind the house loomed a three-story, modern white structure that looked more like an architect's office than a home. It was the only house with another structure in its backyard among the row of houses along the cliff's edge.

"Is *that* also part of your house?" Sage pointed upward at the large white structure.

"Yup. It's my mom's lab."

Mel and Sage gawked, and Lewis laughed. "My mom's a marine biologist for the government. We got permission to have her lab next to our house since we're close to the sea, and it's easy for her to set sail straight from here whenever she needs to. Let's see if she's home so she can help you both get back to your sector."

Lewis brought them through the front door. It was an open-concept floorplan that led straight into the living room with plush couches and an ornate brick fireplace. The dining table was to the left with the kitchen and a large marble island at the far end of the house. Lewis had walked straight toward the kitchen and looked back at them. "My mom's not home right now. Her keys aren't on the kitchen island where she usually places them, so I think she stepped out to her work office."

"She's not at her lab?" Sage asked, nodding to the white megalithic structure through the kitchen window.

"No, her keys would be here if she were at the lab, too. Lab entry is a biometric hand scan. She has another office at the government building."

Sage shot Mel a look as if saying, "Who is this boy, and why do they have a biometric hand scan access in a backyard lab?" Mel, too, was trying to hide her surprise.

Lewis took off his navy suit jacket and laid it across the living room couch that was pristine other than an open magazine splayed on it. "We can wait for her to get back. In the meantime, I can give you a house tour if you'd like."

"Sure." Mel tentatively followed Lewis as he led them up the stairwell between the kitchen and living room. Sage followed behind them. Although the exterior of Lewis's house looked traditional, the interior was quite modern and matched the aesthetic of the lab out back more.

"The upstairs has our bedrooms and my dad's study," Lewis explained as they got to the top of the stairwell.

"Feel free to look around. I'm going to change out of my school uniform." He entered the nearest room to their left and shut the door.

Mel and Sage walked down the hallway at a loss for what to do as they waited. The next room had its door open and displayed a massive king-sized bed and wall shelves filled with plants. *Probably Lewis's parents' bedroom.* They kept walking down the hallway. Photos of Lewis, an older lady, and an older girl lined the hallway. There were a few pictures of the lady with a man and a baby girl, but none of Lewis with the man.

"It looks like Lewis's dad isn't in a lot of these photos," Mel observed out loud.

"It looks like Lewis has a sister!" Sage responded back. The next room also had its door open and a twin-sized bed against the wall. The wall had numerous framed awards, certificates, and curiously, a familiar-looking yellow poster boasting in large letters: *Memory fades, but Reminserum is forever.*

"Sage, I think we saw that same poster in the park," Mel started to say. By now, Lewis had come up behind them. He had changed into a T-shirt and athletic shorts.

"Welcome to my sister's room. And yes, you likely saw that same poster somewhere else. It's the government's poster, and my sister and a lot of the city are obsessed with it."

"I knew from the pictures it was a sister!" Sage applauded herself. "Where is she?"

"She's at school right now, and she's a star student. Hence, all those awards she has up there." Lewis walked past them and farther down the hall to the last room. "This last room is my dad's study. It's my favorite place in the house." He twisted the doorknob and opened the door, inviting them in. Upon entering, Mel saw a table with a lamp and papers strewn across it. Walls of shelves filled with books and strange instruments lined the entire room.

"Wow. What does your dad do?" Sage asked with the same wonder as Mel.

"My mom tells me Dad was an engineer of sorts. These are all his studies and plans." Lewis nodded toward the worktable, and then his expression saddened. "I never knew my dad, though. He disappeared when I was young, and we haven't seen him since."

No wonder there weren't many photos of Lewis with his dad in the hallway.

"It's okay, though." Lewis tried to sound cheerier. "It's been many years. I think my mom keeps his study as it is, hoping he'll return someday. In the meantime, I like to go through his notes and journals. He worked on the government's Memory Rooms, so it's super neat reading about how they work!"

"What's a Memory Room?" Mel's curiosity had her blurt out the question, and she immediately regretted that she'd done what Sage usually would as Lewis gave her a funny look.

"You don't know what a Memory Room is? It's the place all adults use at least once a week because they lose their Kanperetinentia. Memory Rooms are government-sanctioned memory-enhancement aids. The poster you saw in my sister's room? It refers to Memory Rooms. Schools are supposed to teach us about it to prepare us to start using them too once we're eighteen."

"Kanpe—what?" Sage interjected about that word they'd never heard of. Mel was annoyed Sage spoke without thinking again, but she was also too curious about that disease-sounding term to say anything.

"Your parents have never talked about Kanperetinentia or visiting a Memory Room?" Lewis turned to face them fully and crossed his arms.

"No, they never said anything about it," Mel bravely answered to back Sage. "I feel like our parents sometimes don't tell us everything."

Lewis eyed them for a moment. "Well, I suppose I relate with that. I think my mom keeps some things from me too. Adults can be quite secretive sometimes, and they don't realize we're more observant than they think. Since my mom works for the government, and I read my dad's notes, I know quite a bit about all of this, so you're in luck. Kanperetinentia describes the fact we have perfect memory. A Memory Room is a place adults need to use at MAGMA regularly to refresh their memories."

"Refresh their memories?" Sage echoed.

"Yeah. Because we have perfect memory, our brains can't hold that much capacity as we get older, and we start having recall issues because those brain synapses get worse and worse. Our memories become increasingly fragmented as we grow older. So, for example, my memory retention is better than my mom's. Once we hit eighteen years old, we start having memory recall issues, so we need Memory Rooms to help us recall things."

"You all have perfect memory? Like photographic memory?" Sage asked in shock.

"Yes," Lewis paused, "*we,*" he moved his hands in a circular motion as if to encompass all of them in the room, "all have a photographic memory of every detail, speck of dust floating, and word spoken that we can revisit. Give me a time, a day, even the millisecond, and I can pinpoint where I was at that moment and recall it in detail. That's Kanperetinentia," he concluded as if the term explained itself. "But as the brain ages, we'll all need Memory Rooms."

"Which are at a place called MAGMA?" Mel tentatively asked.

"Yes. It stands for 'Multiplex Archive—Government Memory Association,' but that's way too long to remember, so we all call it MAGMA for short. There are MAGMA buildings everywhere, and people can just go in and use the facilities. But people get busy, and it is a hassle to make a trip for everything we have to remember, so many adults simply depend on their children to remind them of events or schedules."

That would explain why those toddlers at the park were so strange! It seems the children here are more mentally developed and can help remind their parents of happenings. Mel's eyes widened in realization.

Sage had walked to the side of the room, tapping a gadget on the shelf as she'd lost interest. But Mel wanted to learn more.

"And MAGMA is government-owned?"

"Yeah, it's owned by the Government Memory Association. The GMA. They run everything memory-related. My mom works for them. Her research with jellyfish is pivotal to memory retention and recall. *Multiplex Archive* is the name of the building that has the Memory Rooms, but *MA*," Lewis made a face of exasperation as he exhaled the term with extreme emphasis, "for short didn't sound

so great, so they just attached their own name to the end
to it to make *MAGMA.*"

Mel laughed. *MAGMA 100 percent sounds better than
just pronouncing the first two letters.*

Lewis smiled at making her laugh. "Do you want to
see the jellyfish my mom works with?"

"Yes!" Lewis had caught Sage's attention while she
was looking through the books and knickknacks on the
shelves. "Why does she work with jellyfish again?"

"She's a marine biologist, remember?" Mel reminded her.

"That's right. My mom's a marine biologist. And
the jellyfish toxin is a natural memory aid. GMA har-
nesses that ability for the Memory Rooms because, in
addition to the room, you will need the memory serum
called Reminserum."

"So, that's what the posters are referring to?" Mel
thought back to the yellow posters.

"Yeah, because the serum helps recall fading memories!" Lewis stopped before speaking again. "I thought it
was common knowledge that jellyfish toxin helps with
memory. It's at every aquarium and museum if you read
the plaques."

Sage shrugged as she placed a book back in its place
on the shelf. "I just look at the exhibits. I don't typically
read through everything." Mel thought to herself that
Sage wasn't lying—she *did* zoom through museums back
at home. *Home!*

Mel remembered they needed to get home. And the
more they spoke with Lewis, the more she didn't want
to speak with his mom, who worked for the GMA. She
would know Mel and Sage were not from around here.
"Actually, Lewis, can we see the jellyfish some other time?

I'd love to see it, but I realized it's getting late, and we need to get back." Sage's head sharply turned toward Mel's direction, about to mouth protest, but Mel scowled at her, so she kept quiet.

"Oh, sure." He seemed a bit crestfallen. "But I thought we were waiting for my mom. She can help get you both back to your sector."

"Oh, no need, Lewis! I think if we can return to the park, we'll be able to retrace our steps and get back," Mel hurriedly responded. "We don't want to trouble your mom. She seems very busy."

"I don't think she'll mind, but sure, I can get you both back to the park. Since it's getting a bit late, it'll be faster to take the bus. I'll take you both to the bus stop just a block from my house."

"Thanks, Lewis." Mel was glad he didn't ask more questions. Mel and Sage made their way downstairs as Lewis carefully closed the door to his dad's study.

"I wanted to see the jellyfish!" Sage was upset.

"It's getting late, Sage. And did you not hear that his mom works for the government? I, for one, don't want to talk to a government person in this strange place. I'd rather get out of here before she gets home," Mel pressed.

Sage thought for a moment. "That's a good point. Mom and Dad are probably worried, too."

Mel nodded. As they got downstairs, however, the front door opened. Mel's stomach dropped with a sense of dread. *We stayed too long... his mom is back!*

But instead, a girl a few years older than them entered and looked at them with mild confusion.

"Hey, Cartier." Lewis joined them downstairs. "This is Mel and Sage," he quickly introduced them. "Guys, this is my sister."

Sage clapped her hands together in recognition, "With the poster and the awards in her room!"

"You took them to my room?" Cartier demanded of Lewis, but he was unfazed.

"Your door was open, but we didn't go inside," he explained. "Not that there's much in there other than your Prime Minister shrine," he added under his breath.

"It's not a shrine, Lewis. You know everyone loves him and he's done great things for our community," Cartier retorted but seemed satisfied they hadn't set foot into her room. "In fact, it'd do you some good to read Prime Minister Gio's book." She waved a pocket-sized yellow book she was holding in her hand titled, *How to be an Upstanding Citizen.*

Lewis made a gagging sound, but Cartier ignored him and continued, "You know this is required reading next year for you, right?" she scoffed.

"Who's that on the back?" Sage asked. Mel then also caught a glimpse of the beaming face on the back of the yellow book, but when she looked back to Cartier for the answer, Cartier's expression was aghast.

"You don't know who this is?" She flipped the book to the back cover to show the man's face clearly. "Author of this book? Prime Minister Gio? Whose family has been running our society for centuries?"

"Oh, yeah, of course, we know him," Mel fibbed as she remembered where she's seen that radiant face. *It's the same face on all those beverages in the vending machine!*

"All right, enough of your free propaganda, Cartier. We're not interested. We're great citizens already." He waved her off. "How could they know it was the Prime Minister on there with you waving the book around like a fanatic?"

Cartier made to smack him with the book, but he ducked.

"You wouldn't want to foul the Prime Minister's sacred book with violence against your brother now, would you?" he goaded her as he took a large step to the front door and opened it.

"Lewis!" Cartier exhaled in frustration.

"Come on, Mel, Sage!" Lewis beckoned them to the door. Mel didn't want to stay around his angry sister, so they took his cue and ran out the door. He slammed the front door behind them and laughed.

His laughter was contagious, and Mel and Sage found themselves hooting with him as they all skipped down the road away from a yelling Cartier.

"The bus stop is over there." Lewis wiped the tears of laughter from his eyes and pointed to a modern, open structure that had a bench and vending machine underneath.

The three of them slowed to a walk to the bus stop. Mel plopped herself onto the bench, and Lewis remained standing, leaning against the bus stop sign. Sage stopped in front of the vending machine next to the bench, the farthest away from the bus stop sign and Lewis.

"Mel, isn't it funny these machines don't require money?"

"The other vending machine at the park also didn't have a slot for coins or money either, but I thought it was just because it was at a public park," Mel responded.

Lewis snorted.

"What're you laughing at?" Sage snapped her head to face him.

"Have you both been living under a rock? Food and drinks don't cost money. Never did." Lewis received no response from the two as they blankly stared at him, so he cleared his throat. "Ahem, you know... all people are given a quota of food based on mouths to feed, season, and occupation."

More blank stares.

"My mom says that the GMA believes that food is a given right for everyone so the government provides it."

"Do you pay for laptops or toys?" Sage asked.

"Yeah."

"Other things around the house like toilet paper and tissues and pots and pans?"

"Yeah. Just not for food." Lewis shrugged. "It's part of the government's Universal Food Care. How do you not know this?"

Mel chimed in, "Oh... just ignore Sage. She, um, makes bad jokes." Mel couldn't think of any better excuse and hoped Lewis would just ignore their questions.

Sage scowled at her. "Yeah, sorry, bad joke."

From the corner of her eyes, Mel spotted the same yellow poster they'd seen around, but this time with the Prime Minister's face on it, as well. She brought Lewis's attention to it to change the topic.

"So, this Prime Minister. He's everywhere. And on your sister's book. Is he popular?"

"Yes, he's a prolific man. He started Universal Food Care and spearheaded funding for the development of Reminserum, which my mom helped with. He's always helping people and creating policies to better our society and for harmony. I respect his work, but many take it too far, in my opinion, and almost worship him. Cartier's an example of that, and she's not even the most intense of them all," he explained and then suddenly furrowed his brows and looked away.

"What's wrong?" Mel asked in concern.

He looked back at Mel with bewilderment. "Well, I was wondering why I was explaining all this to you. The enforcer thing earlier? Sure, every enforcer is different. But our Prime Minister? Everyone knows the Prime Minister."

Mel took a big gulp. Sage, however, was annoyed at Mel for the earlier pitiful excuse she'd made on her behalf and was angrily pressing buttons on the vending machine. "Ugh, nothing's coming out."

Lewis moved his questioning eyes from Mel and addressed Sage, "Sometimes you have to kick it a bit. Some of these machines are a bit finicky."

Mel was glad Lewis got distracted and didn't care to pry about them for now. Sage, meanwhile, was still pressing random buttons on the machine in frustration. "A kick, you say?" She brought her right foot back and jammed it at the bottom of the machine, and Mel immediately lost vision.

She felt as if someone had just thrown her to the floor and had the sensation of being compressed and twisted again. There was no air, and it was dark. *Fwoomp.* Mel felt the impact, and someone was fiercely shaking her.

"Mel, Mel! We're back. We're back home!" Sage was exclaiming.

Mel looked up and saw they were indeed back next to the rice fields and broken vending machine. The one streetlamp had flickered on as it was getting dark.

She sat up, looked at Sage, and hugged her close. After a few moments, they got up.

"You were there with me, right?" Mel patted some grass off Sage. Sage nodded silently. "Let's not tell Mom and Dad. They wouldn't believe us anyway, and I don't want to worry them or have them laugh at us."

"I agree," Sage responded. "I wonder if we can get back there—"

"Are you joking? I want nothing to do with that!" Mel interrupted as she brushed the dirt off herself. Before Sage could respond, Mel's cellphone rang to her shock. *I thought it was dead when I checked earlier at that park. But I can't think about that right now. Mom* flashed on the exterior screen of the phone. Mel looked at Sage and put her index finger to her mouth, signaling Sage to stay quiet. She flipped open her phone.

"I've been trying to call you, Mel! I even called the animal shelter, and they said they hadn't seen you! Is Sage with you? Where are you? Dinner's waiting!"

Relief washed over Mel as she heard her mom's voice. She also had forgotten she was supposed to volunteer today at the animal shelter until her mom mentioned it.

"Yes, Sage is with me. We just took a walk after school and got a little lost."

"Lost? Are you okay? I'm coming out to get you both." Her mom's voice raised in a slight panic.

"No! Mom, I mean, it's okay. We're fine. We found our way back. We're familiar with the area around our school. We're on our way back. I think about thirty minutes? We're literally next to the school," Mel hurriedly responded. She didn't want their parents to find they had wandered out to the fields. Fortunately, there was some truth to what Mel said. The fields weren't too far from Old Town as it was still in view, and Old Town wasn't far from school. *If we do a jog or power walk, we should be home within thirty minutes.*

"Mom!" Sage spoke loudly into the phone while Mel still had it held up to her ear. "We're just exploring around the school. We're coming back!"

"All right. It's not too late out, so get back before it gets dark. Just make sure to pick up my calls, or you won't get off so easy next time!" their mom chided before hanging up. Mel and Sage exchanged glances.

"Let's go home," Sage said as she picked up her book bag from the ground and refastened the buckle.

Mel took a deep breath. "Yes, let's go home."

CHAPTER 4

Dinner was ready when Sage and Mel got home. Out of breath from running the whole way, Mel unslung her book bag onto the living room couch before sitting down at the dinner table. Dinner was eerily quiet, with just the intermittent clinking of utensils on bowls and plates. But Mel could tell from her dad's darkened expression that he was ready to start a tirade at any moment.

Mel saw Sage pick up her glass of water for a sip, and they made eye contact. Mel tipped her head slightly while switching eye contact between Sage and the cup, trying to telepathically tell her, "Put the cup down. Gently. Gently!" Sage very slowly moved the glass from her face to the table, as if the speed could help, but slightly lost grip of the glass and placed it on the table with a clunk.

The trigger.

"What *were* you two thinking?" Dad burst out. "Not a call. Not a text. The volunteer shelter didn't know where you were. The school had no idea where you were. We didn't know where you were!" There was a pause as he gathered himself, and Mel wasn't sure if it was an opportunity to speak or to keep waiting, so she kept silent for now. Mom also had a stern expression to indicate she shared Dad's sentiment. "A phone is a privilege, and we told you to use it to communicate. We trust you two, but instead, you both run off and don't tell us anything!"

Mom put a hand on Dad's hand that was on the table. "We were worried sick. We were just about to call the police if you didn't end up picking up our twentieth call," she added calmly.

"Did you hear your mom? We were about to call the police! Anything could have happened to you! You could have been kidnapped or picked off the roads. And what do you do? You turn off your phones, so we couldn't even pin your location! What are you hiding?"

Mel couldn't stay quiet at that accusation and butted in. "We didn't turn off our phones! I tried using it, but..." She trailed off as she realized she was about to tell them the phone didn't work in the strange place they had visited.

"But what?" Dad glowered.

"It... it didn't work... for some reason." Mel lowered her head.

"What do you mean 'it didn't work'? It's supposed to work. And then what? It miraculously starts working again?"

"It's true, Dad!" Sage added. "Our phones didn't work there!" Mel shot her a look.

"Where, huh?" Dad raised a brow while still having them furrowed.

"Around the fields!" Mel interrupted before Sage said much more. "We were kind of far from town in the fields. We're sorry about that," Mel added morosely. "But we didn't purposely turn off our phones!" Mel's voice teetered on ferocity and desperation for her parents to believe them.

"I think some areas out there are dead zones, honey," Mom interjected.

"But both Mel's and Sage's phone?" Dad's tone softened when addressing their mom.

"Perhaps. Technology isn't always so reliable these days. You know that," Mom said with a slight smile of curiosity. "My father had mentioned the rice fields around the bus stop out there were always kind of wonky."

"Grandpa hung out around there?" Sage asked with widened eyes. *But wait. We didn't mention the bus stop,* Mel thought.

"He did. Our whole family grew up here. Your great-great-grandparents were all farmers around here. And your grandfather was the first to move closer into town. He thought there was better business with carpentry and woodworking here." She put a hand to her mouth as if whispering to the girls. "Said town folks don't know how to fix or take care of their own houses like the people in the countryside do. So that's endless amounts of work for him!"

Sage and Mel laughed. When Grandpa was alive, he always complained about "town folks" not being self-sufficient and working away in his workshop. Who knew he recognized the root of his complaints was his livelihood!

At the laughing of his children, Dad's brows lifted out of the scowl, and he heaved a huge sigh. "All right, all right. Your mom and I were very worried, especially when no one knew where you were. Try not to wander around, especially if you're supposed to be somewhere, and make sure your phone's always charged. If this happens again, we'll have to get them checked, and you'll be in big trouble."

Sage jumped up and hugged Dad and Mom. "Love you, Dad, love you, Mom!"

Mom laughed, and Dad grunted an acceptance, but Mel saw the corners of his mouth lift up.

Sage and Mel cleaned up the dishes after dinner as recompense and then headed back to their rooms.

"Mel, come here for a moment. I need to talk with you," Mom called from the garage. Sage looked back at Mel from the stairwell to their rooms, and Mel gave a shrug. She knew Sage wanted to talk about what happened today in the fields, but that would have to wait.

"Coming, Mom!" Mel turned toward the garage.

***

Mel heard the sounds of boxes shuffling and a clattering of items before she even reached the garage. When she got there, piles of boxes on shelves at one side of the garage surrounded her mom. Their family treated half the garage as storage while reserving the other half for one car. For a clear delineation, her dad had placed shelving down the center of the garage to create a little alleyway on the other side of the shelf. Even then, Mel wondered how the piled junk didn't manage to topple off the shelves into the car's space.

"Over here, Mel," Mom called behind the shelf of boxes.

"What is it?" Mel stepped past the shelf to find her mom rummaging through a box.

"Aha! Found it!" Mom held up a shining object triumphantly. "A photo album! Who knew it was all in here?" She took out a dusty album before looking at Mel. "Do you remember Grandpa? I know he passed when you were quite young."

Mel thought for a moment. "I remember him, but just barely. I remember he always smiled and had funny stories."

"Yes!" Mom got excited and then suddenly disheartened. "He was always a forgetful dad to myself and your aunts, and we thought it was quirky at the time. Silly Dad! I still remember when he was diagnosed with Alzheimer's in his late forties. I was getting ready to leave for university and felt so horrible I was leaving him." Her voice broke a bit. Mel went over, hugged her mom's left arm nearest her, and laid her head on Mom's shoulder, but then her mom took a big sniff as if sucking up all her tears and continued. "After that, as he lost more and more of his memories, he started telling these wild stories and wandering off. Do you remember where he'd wander off to?"

Mel lifted her head and looked at her mom with widened eyes. "The fields. He sometimes took me along!"

"Yes! And I could never reach his cell phone when he was out there. I thought that's why he liked it out there. To be unplugged and get away from the city. In the end, some people in the town would call him crazy because he'd babble tales of a world with free food, giant seals, magic jellyfish, and purple crackers."

It was like Mom had tapped into a forgotten memory. As she talked, Mel remembered some of these stories, and her heart started thumping faster. Not because she remembered these long-ago stories, but because she realized some of these stories sounded like Lewis's world. *The magic jellyfish? It sounds like it could be the memory serum Lewis's mom works on...*

Mom continued her monologue. "It got really bad near the end. He'd ask us where he was and often leave the house in a hurry, walking through town mumbling something about how someone's coming for him and he has to hurry. Our neighbors weren't very kind about that, so we moved to the suburbs. We used to live around Old Town, you know? That part of Old Town has since been torn down for newer buildings. I think it's the post office now." Her mom looked off in thought, probably trying to pull a mental map of the area. "But anyway!" She snapped her attention back to Mel. "When you and Sage mentioned the fields and how you didn't have signal out there, it reminded me of when Grandpa would go out there for hours at a time, and he'd sometimes bring you when you were a wee little thing." She pinched Mel's nose with her free hand.

"Mom!" Mel exclaimed with annoyance and pulled her head back, letting go of her mom's arm. "You know I don't like when you do that!"

Mom laughed, "I know, I know. Take a look at this, Mel." She'd opened the dusty album, and the spine crackled in delight at being given attention. "These are old pictures of Grandpa and Grandma when they were younger. After he passed, Grandma couldn't bear it and followed him peacefully in bed. I still miss them a lot." Mom got pensive again but kept flipping the pages.

Mel saw a picture of two little girls. "Mom, is that you and Auntie?" She pointed.

"Oh, yes, it is. Look at us! We kind of look like you and Sage, huh?"

Mel wrinkled her nose but looked closer and had to admit, other than the different clothing and her mom's and aunt's super short hair, they kind of did look like herself and Sage.

The two of them flipped through the pages, following the growth of Mom. It was neat for Mel as she heard stories she didn't know about Mom, her grandparents, and her aunt. However, as they finished and flipped to the end, Mel saw the corner of a photo tucked into the sleeve of the album at the very back.

"Wait, Mom. What's that?"

Her mom paused at closing the album. "Huh, I'd never noticed that before." She slipped it out to reveal a photo that seemed to have been folded and reopened several times. It was a group photo of quite well-dressed people, and everyone was in long trench coats. Both Mel and her mom brought their heads closer to the photo to scan the faces.

"I found him! Grandpa's there! That's Grandpa, right?" Mel pointed at a young man standing in the back at the edge of the photo, smiling widely.

"Well, that sure is! Good eye, Mel!"

"What do you think this is?"

"I don't know. Grandpa never talked about his life before he met Grandma, honestly. Maybe this is his trade school class. What a neat find, Mel!"

Mel was still looking at all the faces in the photo. There must have been about forty people in the photo, and there were some seemingly important ones sitting in chairs at the very front, but she couldn't help noticing the handsome lady in the tight bun standing next to the seated people. The lady had a hand on her waist and the other resting on a seated person, exuding confidence and authority while also compassion with her eyes that wrinkled with her grin. Mel could see some other members of the group looking at that lady while laughing or smiling. *It looks like she had a lot of influence. And that people really liked her.*

"I think I'll leave the album here," Mom interrupted Mel's thoughts as she closed the book. "It's quite old, and I don't want to risk it falling apart, but it's here if you ever want to take a look."

"Thanks, Mom. That was cool to see. I don't really remember Grandpa because I was so young before he passed, but I remember I liked him."

"Oh! I'd almost forgotten." Mom reached into her pocket and pulled out the shiny object she had previously triumphantly held up upon finding it in the same box as the album. "I got so carried away with the photos that I forgot I came here to find this. Hold out your hand." Mel did as instructed, and Mom placed a small metal key with a long chain onto her palm. Mel looked at it for a moment before looking back at Mom.

"A key?"

"Not just any key, though. This key is something Grandpa always carried. He wore it around his neck, and during one of his periods of clarity, he took it off and told me to pass it to you someday. Your talking about the fields reminded me as it's been in this box ever since. I know it's not much, and no one knows what it's for. But he wanted you to have it, and I hope it's something you can remember him by." Mom looked at Mel tenderly.

"Oh, thanks, Mom."

"Well, put it on! Put it around your neck," Mom urged.

"I don't know, Mom. It's kind of... It doesn't really match my aesthetic." Mel hesitated. She didn't want to wear an old key, but Mom looked at her imploringly, so she put it on.

"Aw, it looks great." Her mom stood up. "Keep it safe! Now, head on to bed."

Mel also got up and ran back into the house. "Thanks for Grandpa's key, Mom! Goodnight." She couldn't wait to share with Sage the tidbit about Grandpa's crazy stories of magic jellyfish and that he often went to those fields. *Perhaps... and just perhaps, Grandpa's stories weren't crazy. Perhaps, they were true.*

CHAPTER 5

Mel went back upstairs, twirling the key around her neck with wonder. *I have to tell Sage!*

She entered her sister's room.

"You didn't knock," Sage said crossly.

Mel waved her off. "Look what Mom just gave me." She took the key off from around her neck and handed it to Sage.

"What's this? Looks old."

"Mom said it used to belong to Grandpa! And he often hung out in the fields and said crazy things about another world with jellyfish and purple crackers..."

Sage clapped a hand to her mouth. "Do you mean...?"

"Grandpa might be from there! Yes!" Mel got excited. "Or at least, he's been before. She said he always carried this key around, so it must be important."

Sage thought for a moment before grabbing her laptop to sit on the bed her sister was on. "I was thinking about everything we saw. The tiny kids talking all weird and smartly. The police officers in purple Barney suits."

Mel stifled a laugh thinking of the purple, goofy dinosaur. "The enforcer's uniform wasn't a Barney suit! It was more burgundy and just... different."

Sage laughed. "Anyway. I thought all the stuff Lewis said about the place was really interesting. And, I think we stumbled into another universe."

"Another universe? Like a parallel universe?"

Sage opened her laptop, turned it toward Mel and herself so they both faced the screen, pulled up a search browser, and typed in: *How many alternate universes are there?*

"I've been doing some research, Mel."

"By doing searches on public databases? If this is real, this information would be classified by the government. That means top secret files locked away in some encrypted place," Mel interrupted, but Sage ignored her.

"There are forums and physicist blogs. People say it's not fantasy. It could be a," she cleared her throat and put on a serious, didactic air, "legitimate theoretical possibility." She went back into her normal voice to add, "There are studies that look into quantum fluctuations, whatever that means, that can create a multiverse!"

"Multiverse?" Mel echoed.

"Multiple universes, duh," Sage chided. "Anyway, from what I'm seeing, it looks like it's possible for there to be other worlds. And I think we stumbled into one, and with this key that you got from Grandpa, perhaps he wasn't crazy! Maybe he went to the same place we went to."

A link on multiverses caught Mel's eye, so she reached for the trackpad and clicked on it. "Each fluctuation could be a different universe with its own specific and unique laws and properties, huh? And there could be millions of possibilities, innumerable of which may even be imperceptible by humans?" Mel read out loud. *Fascinating!*

Sage turned serious. "I think we should go back. To figure out what happened to Grandpa."

Mel looked down. "I'm also really curious about Grandpa. And if he truly wasn't crazy, I'd want Mom to know too. He's such a mystery." She turned toward Sage. "But also, didn't that memory serum and government stuff sound weird when Lewis told us about it?"

Sage put a hand to her chin in thought. "I agree it sounded funny when we first heard. But they have memory issues, and it sounds like the government helps them with that."

"Yeah, that's true." Mel had forgotten people in that world seemed to be wired differently from them. "But I also think we're getting a bit ahead of ourselves. We barely know anything about that place we went to. What if people in that world find out and invade our world?"

Sage guffawed, "I think you've watched one too many movies, Mel! Lewis was nice, wasn't he? And even the enforcer who asked us questions—Lewis said the enforcer is super nice and takes his job seriously. Plus, the government provides free food. You think those kinds of people would invade us?" She eyed Mel dubiously.

Mel thought Sage had a fair point, but she had always been the more cautious, risk-averse out of the two of them and was hesitating.

"Aren't you curious what that key does?" Sage tried another angle.

Mel looked at her and saw her grinning. She knew she had Mel hooked. "Okay, let's check out that vending machine again in the morning before school. Maybe this key fits in something."

Sage fist-pumped the air. "Awesome," she sang.

CHAPTER 6

The next morning, Mel dressed and ran downstairs to grab a toast, only to be surprised Sage was already in the kitchen and had made them peanut butter and jelly sandwiches.

"Ready!" she said as she saw Mel.

Mel shushed her and looked around for Mom and Dad.

"They're still washing up, don't worry. Let's go before Mom and Dad ask us more questions," Sage followed up unconcernedly.

"Okay, sounds good." Mel breathed a sigh of relief. "I'll send them a text that we're leaving earlier to meet for school group projects." She whipped out her phone as they both headed to the front door.

"Mom, Dad! We're heading to school early. Talk to you later!" Sage yelled, completely ignoring the need for stealth, and they ran out. After they were a few blocks from their house, they stopped and took out the sandwiches for breakfast as they walked toward Old Town and the fields.

Old Town wasn't bustling as it was yesterday after school. Most stores were dark as they weren't open yet. Occasionally, there was one person inside their dark store sweeping or setting up. A quiet "good morning" here and there when they passed someone running an early morning errand, but for the most part, it was still and serene.

Mel and Sage finally got to the edge of Old Town to hit the fields and arrived at the bus stop with the vending machines. Everything looked the same.

Sage started searching. "What do you think we did last time to get it to work? To portal us to that other place?"

Mel clicked on a few buttons on the keypad. "I don't know. I think we pressed buttons, but I don't remember exactly which letters or numbers we did."

Sage suddenly kicked the vending machine aggressively.

"What are you doing?" Mel demanded. "You'll break it!"

Sage looked at her. "Have you *seen* this machine? Pretty sure I can't break it much more than it already is. But also, we kicked it last time, so I wanted to try. Do you feel anything funny happening?"

Mel closed her eyes. "Nope. Nothing."

"Hmm, there's got to be something to start it. Maybe it's the drinks vending machine." Sage started examining the functioning beverage machine next to it.

Mel, meanwhile, stood back and looked at the old machine with the funny snacks again. She decided to go to one side of it and feel around the back when she suddenly felt a flap. "Sage, I think I found something."

"What? What is it?"

Mel lifted the flap she felt. "It seems to be an opening. I think I can reach inside it."

"Be careful," Sage said quietly.

Mel had reached inside. "There's something round in here." She fumbled with it as she couldn't quite grab it with just her fingertips, but suddenly, the machine groaned and whirred. Mel pulled back her hand in shock and knocked into Sage in the process. "What was that?"

"Ow, Mel. I don't know," Sage responded as she pushed Mel off her. "I think it started working?"

They both looked at the front of the old vending machine and saw the lights were now curiously on.

"Whoa! How did you do that, Mel?"

"I'm not sure. I just moved a thing around inside, but I couldn't really grab it either."

Sage stopped listening, though. She was now thoroughly looking at the buttons of the selection pad as if hoping they'd divulge which of them was the secret to activating the portal to another world.

Mel scanned the machine and noticed a keyhole that opened the machine to collect the coins that had gone inside. She remembered she had Grandpa's key. A key he held all the time, and he often hung out here. She took the key hanging off her neck out from under her shirt and looked at it.

Could it be?

She brought it closer to the keyhole and Sage noticed.

"Wait a moment. Do you think Grandpa's key is for that?"

Mel shrugged. "Worth a shot, right?" She brought it up to the keyhole and inserted it. *It fits!*

She twisted it, and suddenly, the world pressed in on them. She felt the same feeling of the air getting pushed out of her body as it compressed. She opened her mouth to breathe, but nothing came in. Panic crept in as her chest tightened and her head screamed. And just as suddenly, she landed on the ground again.

CHAPTER 7

"We're back… it worked!" Sage shook Mel.

Mel sat up. *I'll never get used to that feeling right before this happens.* They were back in that park, next to the water fountains, restrooms, and vending machine.

"I don't feel well," Sage added as she rose to her feet.

"That's because you stood up too quickly!" Mel also felt quite nauseous even while still sitting.

Sage teetered toward the park bench when Mel remembered the vending machines didn't cost anything.

"Sage, go get us a drink."

"No, go get it yourself." Sage mustered weakly as she finally made it to the bench and sat.

"No, Sage, it helped us last time to drink something. Go get some. I don't think I can get up this time without throwing up." The image of Sage running to the public restroom last time with the sounds of retches intruded into Mel's thoughts. She tried to push it away lest she started gagging.

Sage got up with a grunt and stumbled to the machine with cartoonishly huge effort. "All right, all right. I'll try this orange drink." She clicked the button assigned to the drink. The machine pushed the selected drink out from its shelf. Sage grabbed it from the machine slot and took a gulp. "Ylech!" she exclaimed. "It tastes like celery and carrots!" Mel took a quick look as she finally managed to get up and walk to the machine.

"No, duh, Sage. It says 'vegetable' on here. Don't you see the pictures of carrots on the packaging?"

"Not with that prime minister's face on it," she said with a humph. Mel turned the drink around and found that same beaming face plastered on it. She rolled her eyes but also took a swig of the drink, hoping it'd help with the dizziness. Sage watched her expression change from annoyance to disappointment.

"Not that great, right?" Sage said.

"Not at all. But also, my head doesn't feel much better either. This drink sucks," Mel agreed.

"What did you get for us last time we were here? It definitely was not this vegetable abomination." Sage stuck out her tongue in disgust.

Mel squinted at the vending machine as she focused on the display inside. "I think it was this one." She pointed at the clear drink option. Another indication was that it was the only drink *without* the Prime Minister's face on it.

"Mensen?" Sage read the label and selected the item.

Upon drinking it, the color immediately returned to Sage's face. "This is it!" She handed it to Mel. Mel weakly took it, put it to her mouth, and tipped her head back. The sweet carbonation hit her tongue, and she immediately felt more clearheaded.

"Ah! You're right. This is the one." Mel took several more gulps. "This stuff is also pretty tasty."

They both took turns with the drink until they finished it and tossed it in a trash bin. Mel noticed there was no one at the park other than a jogger in the distance. In fact, it was still slightly dark, with the sun peeking through the clouds.

"I think it's also still morning here. No one's out yet."

Sage did a sweeping look at their surroundings before responding. "Yeah, it seems the time of day here is similar to the timing at home. What should we do next?"

"Wait!" Mel reached out and grabbed Sage's arm. "Even though there's no one around, I don't think we should wander without a plan. Just because no one's around doesn't mean enforcers may not be around."

"So, what do you suggest?" Sage turned to her and crossed her arms.

"I suggest you think more before doing!" Mel was getting annoyed. "Ugh, I didn't expect us to get back here so soon! I didn't think of a plan." She waved her arms in the air in frustration.

"Mel, you're such a straight edge. Not everything in life needs a plan. We also can't take forever trying to think of one. Let's take a look around. I also made sure to charge my phone so we can maybe film it for research or call someone." Sage took her cell phone out of her pocket and flipped it open, only for Mel to see her face fall. "Huh, it doesn't work. I charged it last night!"

Mel took her own out and flipped it open. Just as Sage said, the phone remained dark. "Mine, too. Maybe our phones don't work in another universe. But a nonworking phone makes me feel kind of naked."

Sage nodded in agreement. "I know you weren't as excited about coming back here. But I agree the fact that our phones just die here is creepy."

"Okay, first things first, we need to find a friendly. Someone on our side. At least we'll be safe with them."

"So, you mean Lewis?"

"Bingo!"

"How do we find him?"

"Probably his house, right? If it's still morning here, maybe he hasn't gone to school yet. But we'll have to hurry to catch him before he goes." Fortunately, Mel had always had a pretty good memory and remembered the general way with landmarks.

"Finally, being on the move sounds good to me." Sage jumped to action like an unloaded spring. "And Lewis had promised to show us his mom's lab! But let's," she turned toward the vending machine again, "grab another Mensen drink. You know, for the road."

***

The two of them power walked. Lewis mentioned there was a bus between his house and the park, and they occasionally saw a bus pass by, but Mel didn't want to risk getting lost. She didn't know what other stops the bus had and the routes it took. She knew this one way to get to Lewis's house, so she was taking this one way to ensure they made it. She also knew following the sound of the crashing waves would lead them closer to Lewis's house on the edge of the cliffs.

They were starting to see more cars on the road by the time they arrived at his neighborhood. The looming white building that was his mom's lab, towering over all the houses in the neighborhood, was a sure sign they were in the right place.

"Amazing, you got us here!" Sage exclaimed and marched toward the front door of the light periwinkle blue house.

"Wait!" Mel burst forward and blocked Sage's way. *I feel like every other thing I say to Sage is 'wait.' She's always rushing off without a second thought!* "We can't just knock on his front door! His mom might be home. She doesn't know who we are, and she works for the government."

"Oh, yeah..." And right on cue, they saw a figure inside walk past the front window.

"Get down!" Mel pulled Sage to the ground as they sprawled in the grass, bellies down.

That same person opened the front door and called toward the back of the house. "Off to school! See you both for dinner!" She didn't see Sage and Mel as they were still on the ground, and she had turned away from them and walked in the opposite direction down the road. Mel and Sage stayed silent until the person was out of sight.

"Was that his mom?" Mel didn't get a clear look at her face.

"She said she's going to school. I think that's his sister, right?"

"Oh, that would make sense." Right at that moment, the front door opened again, sending her heartbeat sky-rocketing once more. Mel wasn't sure if they'd be so lucky not to be sighted this time while sprawled on their lawn, so she motioned to Sage to roll closer to the house and into the bushes that lined the front wall. Sage caught on quickly and they moved.

A boy exited the doorway. "I'm going to school, too, Mom!" He started walking in the direction the girl had gone earlier. Mel stuck her head out of the bushes to call Lewis's name.

"Hold on, Lewis." A woman ran out the door. "You forgot your permission slip for the field trip." Mel froze to avoid rustling or disturbing the bushes.

"Mom, I didn't forget. I don't forget things." Lewis had turned back to face his mom and the house. "I just don't want to—" He paused, and his eyes widened as he saw Mel's head stuck outside from under the bushes, clear as day.

"Lewis?" His mom looked at him questioningly. Mel could only see the back of his mom but saw her readjust her stance to look behind her.

"Mom!" Lewis said loudly to bring her attention back to him. "Normal aquariums are *so* boring! I've seen your lab and tagged along with you to other research facilities ever since I can remember. I'm just not interested in a public citizen's aquarium for this field trip."

His mom gave a light-aired, hearty laugh. "I suppose that's true. You've seen it all and more probably." She stuffed the paper slip she was holding back into her pocket, "I'll keep this then, and you can stay at home that day. I'll let your teachers know."

Meanwhile, Mel was sweating from trying to stay absolutely still and not make a sound. Hiding in the bushes wasn't such a great idea if one had to move around.

"Mel, get back in here!" Sage whispered forcefully from farther in the bushes.

"Shhhh!" Mel managed out of the corner of her mouth, but it wasn't quiet enough.

"What was that?" Lewis's mom turned her head to the side.

"Mom! Hey, I think I forgot a book in your car. Can you help me look for it real quick? I don't want to be late for school," Lewis had rushed forward to his mom before she completely turned around, grabbed her arm, and led her away from Mel and Sage toward the garage.

"Oh, uh sure, Lewis." She let Lewis lead her away. Lewis looked back and gave Mel a nod. "Get out of here!" he seemed to say.

He doesn't have to tell me twice! Mel thought, and once they were out of earshot, she rustled back into the bushes. *We can stay put until everyone's gone or back inside the house.*

"She almost saw you!" Sage said in a hushed tone.

"I know! You didn't have to talk when she was so close!" Mel snapped, and Sage scowled. She was about to deliver a retort when they heard Lewis's voice in the distance.

"Thanks, Mom! Turns out, it was already in my backpack! Silly me. I'm off then!"

"You shouldn't be having memory issues yet, Lewis! I don't know what you're up to but stay out of trouble, and don't be late for lunch!" his mom called back. Lewis's mom came back into view through the bush leaves and returned to the front door. She paused at the doorway, turned around, and peered at the exact bushes where Mel and Sage were hiding with a quizzical expression. Mel felt eyes boring into her through the greenery and held her breath. Lewis's mom stepped toward them when Mel heard a phone ring inside. His mom stopped, looked back inside the house through the front door, then sighed and went inside.

Mel and Sage both exhaled in relief.

"*What* are you two doing here?" Lewis popped his head into the bushes, also sprawled on the ground but outside.

"Ahhh!"

"Oh my gosh!"

Both Mel and Sage yelped in exclamation, and Lewis hastily threw out his hands to cover Mel's mouth as she was closest to him. "Hold on. It's me. It's me! Lewis! Calm down. She'll hear you!" Upon seeing his face, both Mel and Sage immediately quieted down.

"What are *you* doing?" Sage uttered back. "Aren't you supposed to be in school?"

"Not today, apparently, if you two are here. Aren't *you* two supposed to be in school, too?" Lewis repositioned himself, so he was leaning on his forearms. Sage opened her mouth but seemed to think twice about it and closed it to Mel's surprise. Lewis gave a crooked smile, "But first, let's get out of these bushes. My mom's getting ready to go to the MAGMA building and will leave soon, so she won't be at her lab. Let's go there. Follow me." He scooted backward out of the bushes and disappeared.

Mel and Sage exchanged looks before Mel wiggled out of the bushes to follow.

The three of them crept along the house's edge toward the back. Lewis slowly unlatched the gate leading to the backyard to get to his mom's lab. "Stay low," Lewis mouthed to Sage and Mel while gesturing to get to the ground. He crouched on all fours and crawled toward the towering, modern building. Mel and Sage followed suit.

Peeking back at the house, Mel saw windows from the kitchen looking out into the backyard and large glass doors to access the house. The back of the house was almost like a fish tank with the amount of clear glass there. *No wonder we have to stay low here. Hopefully, to stay out of his mom's line of sight if she's there.*

Lewis started running but on all fours, somehow like a four-legged animal, which looked quite bizarrely hilarious with his navy school suit uniform flapping and backpack strapped to his back. Sage gave a snort when he started, and Mel stifled a laugh at hearing Sage trying to contain herself. Given how adept he was, Mel had no doubt he'd probably snuck into his mom's lab multiple times before with this method. Sage and Mel shuffled their knees and hands along the grass as fast as they could to keep up.

They got to the front wall of the white building, and Lewis quickly reached upward from his crouched position to place his hand on a black keypad. Mel saw a red outline quickly sketch his hand and blink green before he removed his hand. Suddenly, cracks emerged from the white wall, outlining a large door. Lewis pushed, and it swung inward. "Inside, quick!" Lewis said as he glanced back at his house. He let Mel and Sage through first before slipping in himself.

When they entered, the interior lit up with ambient lighting to reveal a large conference room with a long table in the middle, numerous plush chairs bordering the table, a screen at the end, and a little kitchenette at the corner for refreshments. A smaller office lined with glass walls was to their immediate right side. It had a desk, chair, photos of Lewis and his sister, and a computer desktop. To their left was a stairwell that went down into darkness.

Lewis had straightened up and headed to the kitchenette in the far corner. "You guys want anything to drink?"

Mel and Sage also stood back up from their crouched positions and straightened out their clothes. Mel saw a few leaves and twigs in Sage's hair and picked them out,

"Hold still, Sage." Then she called out toward Lewis, "No, thank you, I'm fine."

"You sure? There's water, apple juice, assorted teas, Mensen, and coffee, but I don't recommend that unless you want to add a bunch of sugar and dairy in there."

"I want a Mensen," Sage volunteered as she combed out her hair with her hands after Mel finished with her.

"Actually, a Mensen would be nice too," Mel said as she remembered that refreshingly bubbly drink from the vending machine.

Lewis grabbed two bottles from the kitchenette fridge and poured a cup of juice for himself. "Here you go." He handed them their bottles. "Since we're inside the building already, are you both still interested in seeing my mom's lab?"

"Yes!" Sage exclaimed while Mel nodded fervently.

Lewis grinned mischievously. "It's this way." He headed toward the stairwell. "You're both in for a treat. You're about to see the best aquarium you'll ever go to." Mel thought he truly seemed proud of his mom's lab. They followed him down the dark stairwell, but as they walked, the lights along the stairwell turned on to illuminate their path. As they descended, the walls transitioned into glass. Already, they were stepping into the underwater world. The walls were now sequences of curved tanks. There were mollies, guppies, crabs, lobster, and goldfish— different fish in each tank.

"I take care of these just for fun. But you've yet to see my mom's stuff," Lewis said as they headed deeper down. When they finally reached the bottom, the first thing Mel saw was a ginormous stingray swimming along the glass of the floor-to-ceiling tank in front of them. Sage gasped out loud next to Mel. The whole far wall was glass, filled with water of deep blueness, and they'd arrived in a room the size of an auditorium.

"That's Sticky the manta ray." Lewis noticed the stingray too. "He's kind of a show-off," Lewis added, seeing their gaping faces. "He's in the main tank, which is state of the art. It holds approximately 1.5 million gallons, and the acrylic glass is about thirty inches thick. Sticky isn't the only manta ray in there. We have a few more, then some other kinds of stingrays, schools of fish, and some sharks too." As if on cue, a whale shark slowly swam across the front of the tank at that moment. "A lot of them came here for rehabilitation or because they were injured, and depending on how they're doing, my mom may keep them or set them free."

Lewis led them away from the stairs through the room. "Then, we have these other tanks," he waved at the chest-level tanks scattered throughout the huge room, "for smaller fish, plant life, or small sick fish."

Mel shifted her focus to the rest of the room and saw the smaller tanks lining the other three auditorium walls or free-standing in different areas like islands. All those tanks had hoods of lights and tubing above them or connected to something in the tank. They walked past a chest-level tank that looked to hold rocks, coral, and starfish. There was also a section of tubs stacked vertically on shelving, holding plants submerged in water. Another wall section had various devices and nets hung up or on shelves. "Those are plant and animal collecting devices. Or things for sampling water and the seafloor. Plus Mom's diving gear," Lewis said as he saw Sage gravitate toward that wall.

"That door leads to the main lab equipment. Like her microscopes, camera equipment, computers, imaging devices, incubators, and cold storage." Lewis pointed at a door to the side.

"This is incredible." Sage was looking at the large tank in awe.

"Yeah, my mom loves this stuff. But this isn't what she works on for the government at MAGMA. She works on deep-sea animals for that. That's farther down in the building." He headed for another set of stairs under the first one they descended. Mel hadn't seen it since she was distracted by everything else in the room. As they went down, Mel noticed goosebumps on her skin and heard Sage start chattering her teeth.

"It's k-k-kind of c-cold," Sage managed.

"We have to keep temperatures cool for deep-sea creatures, and it makes the whole area a bit colder." They'd reached the bottom of the stairs, and it was noticeably darker here than it was at the aquarium section earlier. Lights lit up as they arrived, but it was dimmer, with less white lighting.

"I can't see anything." Mel squinted while waiting for her eyes to adjust.

"The deep sea is extremely dark because sunlight doesn't reach it, so we have to keep relatively low lighting in here. I like to call this section of Mom's lab, the Midnight Zone. I call the one we just saw earlier the Sunlight Tank. I know I said Sunlight was state of the art, but these tanks in the Midnight Zone are truly state of the art."

"How so?" Mel asked while hugging her body.

"My mom said deep-sea animals are more sensitive, so they're typically harder to keep alive or house. That's why these tanks have filtration technology to pump bone-chillingly cold water with very low oxygen levels to emulate the deep sea. There are chillers somewhere too, keeping everything cold and numerous pressure vessels for smaller deep-sea animals that may need more care."

As Mel's eyes adjusted, she saw that the layout of the Midnight Zone was similar to the Sunlight Tank. The far wall was also a massive floor-to-ceiling tank, but instead of one tank in Sunlight, it was split down the middle into two tanks. The ceiling here was lower, so the tank itself seemed a bit smaller too. Multiple other small tanks with lights, tubes, and equipment lined the room's edges. The animals inside these tanks looked otherworldly. Glowing, floating, soft-looking, squishy. Mel approached one of the smaller tanks on the side of the room, which held a red, bell-like jellyfish. "What is this?"

Sage glanced over. "Looks like a red beret!"

"That's a more recently discovered deep-sea creature," Lewis explained. "Everyone apparently got very excited about it. They're calling it the 'Blood-red jellyfish' for now, but they think it's in the same genus as one other jellyfish. *Poralia rufescens*. But there's some debate, and they're still studying it. Pretty, isn't it?"

Mel couldn't take her eyes off its floating form. "It is. I've never seen a red jellyfish."

"And your mom works in this lab all by herself?" Sage asked, motioning around. "How could she do everything when it's so ginormous?"

Lewis laughed. "Fortunately, no. My mom has interns and other biologists who work here. Her tanks have around-the-clock monitoring and adjusting built in, plus alerts that'll go straight to her. She also has people who help her take care of the tanks and animals, but she doesn't like them being here when she's not, so she arranges for them to come on days she doesn't work at her MAGMA office."

"How often does she work at MAGMA?" Mel wondered out loud.

"Usually, she works from home—here." Lewis gestured to the room. "She only goes into the government office for presentations or to ask for more funding. But she told me she's booked all this week to go in. She said all the higher-ups got in a frenzy over something that happened yesterday, so every government employee has been expected to go in. I hear her complaining on the phone with her friends that she doesn't understand why *she* has to go in, but maybe it's for emergencies or something."

Sage's eyes widened in interest. "Did you hear what happened to make the higher-ups frenzied?"

Lewis shrugged. "No. She said no one knows. Just that she heard down the grapevine something of huge governmental concern happened, and they're doing some damage control. I don't remember my mom having to spend days there before, so I think it doesn't happen often. I wouldn't worry about it, though. The GMA is good at what they do. Anyway, that means no one will be here this entire week except for the evenings when my mom gets back."

"When exactly did she hear she had to go into the office every day again?" Mel asked. She couldn't help but wonder if perhaps it coincided with...

"Yesterday afternoon," Lewis answered. "That's why she wasn't home when you came over then. She had to leave quite suddenly and came back home complaining that she has to be at MAGMA every day now."

Sage and I found ourselves in this odd world yesterday afternoon, too, which means time in this world and time at home runs similarly? And was it a coincidence they called his mom into the office at the same time Sage and I got here?

"Mel, Mel! Are you listening?" Lewis had walked up to her and looked at her questioningly. She snapped out of it.

"What? What is it?" Mel looked over to Sage and could see Sage's worried eyes slightly illuminated by the dim lights.

"I was saying," Lewis continued, "speaking of yesterday..." He looked away for a moment before meeting Mel's gaze again. "Something weird happened with you two." He glanced at Sage too. "We were at the bus stop to get you back to the park, and you both started... flickering."

"Flickering?" Mel echoed. *At the bus stop here... the bus stop! That's when Sage and I somehow made it back home... and Lewis saw it all!* Mel mentally berated herself for not even thinking of how they'd explain that to Lewis. She forgot they were right in front of him when they transported home.

"Yeah. You both froze and flickered. Like one split second you were there, and then you weren't. Rapidly flickering. And you weren't responding to me. It happened so fast that when I reached forward for one of your arms, you both just," Lewis raised his hand and looked at his empty palm, "disappeared."

PART TWO

CHAPTER 8

"Who are you guys?" Lewis took a step forward. "What are you?"

Mel took a step backward, "I—"

"I thought I just dreamed you up when you disappeared. I thought I was going mental. But then you came back! You're here." Lewis turned away and started pacing. "So I thought you have to be real. Then how do I explain the disappearance? You're magical. Wizards? A new government invention on tangible holograms? Or you're creations of competing scientists, sent here to spy on my mom's work?"

"Whoa, hold on, we're not spies!" Sage interrupted. She'd been backing away from Lewis and toward the stairs but had now started marching toward him to confront him. "Call us spies again!" She got up to his face and pressed a finger to his chest.

He looked at her blankly. "Well, I've never seen anything like you both flickering out of existence. You said you're from some school I've never heard of."

"Northridge," Sage reminded him impatiently.

"You've been asking me strange questions about our sector's enforcers, so it seems like you're not from this sector and that you're feeling out our security."

"We're not some scientific tool or creations or spies. Stop making it sound like we're items or here for some dark reason! We're normal human beings!" Sage retorted.

"Normal humans who can blip in and out of places?" Lewis crossed his arms.

"Look, Lewis," Mel interjected. "If we were spies for another scientist, why would we leave in a rush yesterday when you asked if we wanted to see your mom's lab? If we were spies, we'd have agreed and seen it already. Why would we leave right then?" She tried to reason with him.

Lewis thought about it. "That's a fair point. Maybe something urgent happened, and you had to return to your sector. You came back here today, didn't you?"

"Okay, stop saying we're from another sector. We don't even know what sectors are! We're not from here!" Sage said in frustration.

Mel's stomach dropped.

Lewis homed in on that statement. "Not from here, you say?"

"No! We weren't asking about your enforcer in this sector specifically. I have no idea what an enforcer is! He looks like a police officer in weird colors. How do you all have free food? Memory houses? The kids here all talk like they have super brains. We're *not* spies," Sage spewed out in one breath.

"Sage!" Mel said warningly. But it was too late. Sage had said too much.

"Wait. So you both really have never heard of Memory Rooms? Or MAGMA? Or even enforcers?" Lewis had uncrossed his arms.

"Sage—" Mel tried to stop her.

"Mel! We can't have him thinking we're spies!" Sage turned back to Lewis. "No, we don't know any of those things. Not because our parents never told us about them, but because these things don't exist where we're from."

"They... don't exist?" Lewis carefully repeated with a perplexed expression and looked at Mel for confirmation.

Mel took a big sigh. *It's too late anyway. Might as well tell Lewis everything.* He'd also helped them yesterday and today to stay away from other adults. "No, they don't exist where we're from. Everyone just remembers things on their own."

"Don't they have problems recalling memories?"

"Well, yes. Yes, we all do," Mel admitted. "But it's normal for us to forget things. Or remember things wrongly. Our mom and dad sometimes argue because one of them remembered something wrong."

"For example," Sage nodded in agreement, "Mom will think she told Dad to go buy milk from the store, and she'd get upset if he didn't. But then he'll say that she never told him to do that. And it's a whole misunderstanding."

"You can remember things wrongly?" Lewis looked aghast.

"Yes. It's normal," Mel said. "We've had lessons at school about wrong eyewitness accounts putting people into prison just because people remembered incorrectly. Not just that, though. My best friend, Becks, and I sometimes argue over misunderstandings on what we said to each other or just on remembering things we previously did together."

"Wow." Lewis was incredulous. "And your government doesn't help with memory to prevent these misunderstandings that stem from things that were," he paused and looked upward in thought for the right word, "misremembered?"

"No, that's not the point," Mel said. "We don't need the government's help with our memory. Misremembering is just something that happens. Sure, it's horrible that the wrong people can be put in jail or people get in arguments, but it's normal."

"The government can't do anything to help? Why not make sure everyone has accurate memory to prevent these things? If you know these are problems, why is there no solution?"

"Because we all own our own memories!" Sage exclaimed. "We don't need help. We remember things on our own. We have control of our own memories."

"Yeah," Mel added. "There are already issues with online privacy of our information. Governments can't have access to our memories, too. That's a privacy breach!"

"I don't understand why the government can't have access and help you all have clear memories," Lewis said.

"Clear memories?" Sage asked.

"Yes. Clear, accurate memories."

Sage opened her mouth, but Lewis continued, "But I'm more interested in the fact that you're saying you're from a different world. No enforcers, no Memory Rooms, no Reminserum."

"Also, no Universal Food Care. You know how you told us people don't have to pay for food or drinks? People in our world do. People work hard to care and feed their families. Sometimes, homeless people go hungry. Sometimes, people living in areas with no grocery stores nearby have difficulty finding good quality groceries and food. There's famine and hunger in parts of our world. We learn about all of it in history and hear about it on the news."

Lewis's jaw had dropped. "That sounds so stressful. To constantly worry about putting a meal on a table?"

"It's sad to read about and see on the roads," Mel concurred.

"So, your world is completely different. How did you get here?" He looked away and mumbled under his breath, "It's like Dad's notes..."

"We haven't figured that out yet. It happened on accident," Sage answered, and before Mel could ask him what he meant about his dad, a robotic announcement played on the system in the lab.

"Dr. Leo-Trisham entering the building."

"That's my mom!" Lewis yelped in surprise. "She must have come back to grab something she forgot." He started walking toward the side of the room. "Pretty par for the course. It's normal for her to forget items, so she has reminder notes in her car and probably just realized she missed something."

"And the building just announces entry?" Mel said, following him.

"Yes, the system will announce anyone who enters, so anyone in the building is aware. When I entered, the building announced my entry too, but we didn't hear it because we were outside. Stop asking these unnecessary questions. Just come on. We have to hide and turn off the lights! These lights are motion sensor, so if the stair lights are on, she'd know someone's here." Lewis tapped a spot on the wall, and a small panel popped out. He removed it to reveal a series of switches within it.

"Come here and hold onto me. I'm about to kill the lights, so it's about to get even darker."

Mel turned back, held out her hand for Sage, and then grabbed the bottom of Lewis's uniform jacket with her other hand. "Ready."

Lewis nodded and flipped several switches. The lights at the stairwell turned off, and the Midnight Zone was dipped into darkness other than the few lights in some of the tanks, giving the space an eerie undertone. Mel felt Lewis start moving. She clutched his jacket and Sage's hand harder and shuffled forward to follow. They seemed to walk along the wall that had the panel. Lewis then paused, and there was a click and a clunk of something setting onto the floor. A hand grabbed the hand Mel had on Lewis's jacket. "Let go. We're good. Go inside," came Lewis's voice in the darkness, and he pulled her into a small space. She then felt Sage come in and press against her.

"What's this place?" Sage said quietly.

"A hideout in the wall. Just stay quiet," Lewis said behind Sage as he lifted the panel he had removed and put it back in place in front of them. They'd entered an enclave in the wall. At that moment, they heard footsteps run down the stairs they were just on.

"Where did I put those files again?" Lewis's mom's voice was muffled. There was some shuffling of items, more footsteps, and an opening and shutting of a door. The footsteps came dangerously close but then left.

"Hello? This is Dr. Leo-Trisham." *Sounds like she picked up a phone call,* Mel thought. "Yes, I'll be there. I just need to grab something. Oh, oh, it's an emergency? I understand," she said, followed by receding footsteps back up the stairs.

All three of them kept still before Lewis exhaled. "Okay, we're good. Let's get out of here. Mom sounded pretty serious on her phone call just now. If she caught me in here with you two, she would be doubly upset with the mood she's in currently." He pushed the panel back out and helped Sage and Mel step out. The dim lights were back on already from Lewis's mom walking around the Midnight Zone just moments ago.

Lewis carefully placed the panel back into place, creating what looked like a seamless wall. Sage had wandered off to look at a tall tank full of red jellyfish. "Are these Blood-red jellyfish like the one earlier?" she asked.

Lewis looked over his shoulder at them as Mel joined Sage. "No, those are a bit different if you look more closely." Mel could see what Lewis meant when she got closer. Even though they were also red, they seemed like small UFOs—small flying saucers with longer tentacles trailing down. "Those are atolla jellyfish. They're bioluminescent, so if they're alarmed or attacked, it'll flash and look bluer."

"Wouldn't that just draw more attention to it?" Mel asked.

"You're right. And that's exactly the point. It flashes to draw more attention from other predators that may be interested in its attacker. So, a predator can come to chase the attacker, and the jellyfish will be unbothered."

Mel was impressed at that. Lewis had walked up to them now. "Funny that these should draw your attention. These are the main jellyfish toxin we use for deriving Reminserum. These help Memory Rooms function."

"The toxin helps people remember things?" Sage asked, touching the glass.

"Well, I wouldn't recommend touching it. The raw toxin won't help. That's where my mom's research comes in. She helps with extraction and synthesizing it for usage that's safe in unlimited dosages for our minds. They somehow discovered years ago that contact with it could help with memory, and the GMA started research from there and perfected Reminserum. A huge point in our history. Now, come on. Let's leave here for now." Lewis started up the stairs.

Sage took her hand off the glass and followed. Mel took one last look at the floating red saucers, wondering what they'd look like when they flashed, and then followed them up.

They entered the Sunlight Tank room again before continuing up the stairs to the conference room and kitchenette and exited through the front door. Mel watched the door melt seamlessly into the wall as Lewis shut it behind them. He then turned to the biometric keypad and clicked a few buttons. "I'm deleting the log that shows I came in here since I'm supposed to be in school."

"It's that easy to delete the history?" Mel was surprised he could delete it straight from the keypad outside the lab. *Doesn't seem very secure...*

Lewis smiled as he continued pressing a few buttons on the keypad. "Technically, no. The log saves on the main servers within the lab, but everyone's too busy to pull the log all the time. Usually, people will just check here to see who's been in and out or if they can ask someone for something if they've been here recently. I'm just deleting the information locally here."

Something rustled behind them, so Mel turned away from Lewis and the building to face Sage. "Stop messing about, Sa—." Her eyes widened. Sage wasn't there.

***

Where's Sage? Mel didn't see her anywhere in the backyard and immediately ran toward the side gate to the front of the house.

"Where are you going?" Lewis called to her, but she didn't care.

Where did Sage run off to this time? She's always wandering off. Mel was feeling annoyed at Sage's habit. But she didn't see Sage past the side gate nor at the front of the house. She scanned the front porch of Lewis's house and the street in front of it. No sign of Sage. Mel then looked in the bushes they hid in earlier. She wasn't there either. Panic started creeping into Mel's chest.

"Sage?" she called out in a loud whisper. No answer. "Sage!" Mel called out even louder. "Sage! Where are you?" She was now yelling.

"Quiet down! The neighbors will hear you if you're yelling!" Lewis ran up behind her.

"Sage!" Mel paid him no attention. It wasn't like Sage to simply not respond. Even though Sage often went off on her own, she always waited for Mel to catch up.

Lewis turned Mel around and took both of her shoulders. "Mel! Shush! We don't want to draw attention to you. Calm down. Please!"

Mel looked at him and felt a lump form in her throat. "She's not here," she heard an unfamiliar voice squeak out of her mouth.

CHAPTER 9

Lewis looked at Mel with concern as they stood in his front yard.

"She's not here!" Mel repeated with an edge of hysteria. *We're in a different world, of different people, with unknown things. What if something happened to Sage? What do I do? Who do I go to?*

Lewis looked around. "I don't see her either. But she probably isn't far. Let's go inside the house first before the neighbors call Enforcer Jovanna on us again for skipping school." He held Mel's hand to lead her inside the house through the front.

Mel followed in but couldn't stop scanning the neighborhood for Sage's figure. She saw nothing but the pristine lawns of the neighbors' front yards, but when Lewis let go of her hand to unlock his front door, Mel caught sight of a shadow moving quickly farther down the row of houses.

She grabbed Lewis's arm. "Did you see that?"

Lewis turned his head after unlocking and pushing the door. "What?"

"There was something down the road. Moving very quickly."

"Do you think it was Sage?"

"No, I don't think so. It was really brief." At that moment, Sage's voice broke through the air.

"Mel! Run! There's somebody he—" And it went silent. Mel took a moment to process before running toward her voice.

"Sage! Where are you?" She was suddenly pulled into the house. Lewis slammed the door shut and bolted both locks. "What are you doing?" Mel turned to Lewis angrily. "She needs help!"

"She told us to run! We don't know what's out there," Lewis said. Before Mel could argue back, they heard a creaking hinge outside at the side of the house and fell silent.

"That might have been the side gate to the backyard," Lewis whispered.

"Lewis," Mel said quietly, "is the backdoor locked?" His eyes widened, and he bolted to the back of the house. He checked the lock, turned back, and nodded at Mel. "Whew." Mel breathed a sigh of relief.

"I'm going to call my mom and Enforcer Jovanna," Lewis whispered from the back of the house. Both of them stood frozen, facing each other across the first floor, with their backs pressed against the doors. Mel fervently nodded. She didn't care anymore if an enforcer came. If someone could help get Sage back from whatever was out there, she didn't care if she'd get taken to the station or even to jail. They could worry about that later.

"Crud! I left my backpack with my cell phone in the nook at my mom's lab!"

Mel checked her cell phone in her pocket. It was still dark. "Mine doesn't work either."

Lewis looked around and spotted their landline home phone in the kitchen. He pointed to his right. "We can use that." Mel could see the phone hanging not too far on the kitchen wall, but at that moment, she saw a figure streak across the window above the kitchen sink.

"Lewis! It's here! I just saw it again!" She pointed frantically at the window.

"All the doors and windows are locked. It can't get in. I just have to get the phone." He started crawling toward the kitchen when Mel saw a figure with a long coat materialize right outside the glass of the backdoor. She screamed. Lewis hadn't gotten too far from the backdoor and turned to see the figure just outside.

"Oh my gosh!" He collected himself, shakily saying back to Mel, "Don't worry. It can't get inside. Gosh, I never liked these glass doors and windows everywhere."

But then the figure started gliding toward the door with no hesitation. Mel noticed the figure had a fuzzy outline.

"Lewis... Lewis! What is it doing?" Then, right before their eyes, it stepped through the glass into the house! Once it had fully entered, the figure was no longer fuzzy and looked fully materialized.

Both Lewis and Mel yelled at the same time.

How the heck did she get inside?

"Mel, run! Go find Enforcer Jovanna!" Lewis had taken off his shoe, thrown it at the figure, and turned to scramble up and run. The figure immediately lunged at Lewis, tackling him.

"Lewis!" Mel screeched as she watched them tussle, frozen in fear. The figure was clearly overpowering Lewis, and at his shout of pain, Mel jolted back to action. She grabbed an umbrella next to the front door and held it up like a baseball bat. She couldn't leave Sage and Lewis behind.

She could see the humanoid figure more clearly now. It wore a long trench coat with a hood covering its face in shadows. It stood up, holding Lewis in front of its body. A glowing rope snaked up his legs and torso, pinning his arms to his sides and wrapping around his mouth, so all he could do was grunt while struggling fruitlessly.

"You're going to fight me?" a distorted alto voice emitted from under the hood.

"What do you want with us?" Mel yelled back.

Lewis was still grunting, trying to get out of the rope's viselike grip.

The figure laughed. "I like you. You got some moxie. But I need you both to come back with me because I have some questions for you." It took out another glowing rope from inside its trench coat.

Mel thought to herself, *I could make a run for it. I'm right next to the front door, and it's at the back door.* Lewis made a grunt and was making head movements telling Mel to go. *But I can't leave him behind. And Sage. This thing* has *to have Sage too.* Her grip tightened on the umbrella she held. "Give me back my sister! And him!"

"Oh? The little girl before is a sister?" The figure's voice lilted. "I can't give her back. But if you come with me, you can see her."

"No!" Mel screamed while charging forward, umbrella above her head. She swung the makeshift weapon at the figure's head, hoping to make a hit and avoid Lewis standing in front of it, but the figure lazily stepped aside while maneuvering Lewis from behind so he was also out of the umbrella's trajectory. Mel tripped forward, having lost her balance when the umbrella didn't make an impact as she expected. She took a step to regain her balance, but her necklace with Grandpa's key fell out from under her shirt, the morning sun glinting off it.

The figure saw it and gave a commanding, "Wait."

Mel stopped at that and looked toward the figure's hooded head.

"Where did you get that?" The figure had one hand holding Lewis from the back and used its other hand to point at Grandpa's key. Mel looked down at the key hanging off her neck.

"I got it from my mom. What do you want with it?"

The figure fell silent, pausing to think before responding. "I know the original owner of that key. I can tell you more if you come with me."

Grandpa? This thing knows Grandpa? "What about my sister? And Lewis?" Mel challenged. She gripped the umbrella tightly, ready to swing again. She had a feeling this figure could easily disarm and immobilize her as it did with Lewis, but she also sensed that it had a change of heart and no longer wanted to fight.

"Your sister is safe. And I won't harm this one either." It jerked its head in Lewis's direction. "But you need to come with me immediately. It's not safe here."

"Not safe here? Safe from what?" Mel's curiosity was piqued. Lewis, too, had stopped struggling to listen.

"Not here. It's too dangerous. If you don't believe me, I'll say I know the last place I saw the owner of that key around your neck is in a town called Norioh, surrounded by rice paddies."

At hearing the name of her town, Mel started lowering her umbrella. "How do I know you won't hurt us?"

"Do you know what that key does?" the figure inquired.

Mel shook her head.

"I know that to you, there's no guarantee I won't hurt you. I'd have the same question too. But consider your options. Either I tie you up and take you both with me anyway, or you both follow me on your own accord." Mel knew the figure could effortlessly subjugate her. "Look," the figure continued, "I'll let him go, but only if you both promise not to run or try attacking me. I assure you, I can easily wrap you both up in ropes and carry you back with me. So if you'd rather be more comfortable and walk on your own, then no funny business."

It did something behind Lewis's back, and the rope unraveled on its own and wrapped itself around the figure's forearm. Once free, Lewis immediately ran toward Mel, and they both looked back at the figure.

"We need to go now. Follow me." The figure turned toward the back door, unlocked it, and left. Lewis and Mel looked at each other and then followed the figure into the backyard, around the house, and to the street.

Lewis seemed to have regained some courage and whispered loudly to the figure, "Why didn't you just walk through the backdoor like you did before?"

The figure chuckled. "Why do that when I can just unlock the door from the inside? I only do it when necessary." They'd marched down the street and turned a corner. They started walking down a series of stairs carved into the cliffs on which Lewis's house sat, the volume of the crashing waves increasing with each step.

"We're going to the beach?" Lewis asked.

"No more questions. Follow closely." They'd reached the bottom of the cliffs, and from there, Mel could see Lewis's mom's lab towering in the distance above them. Below it, she noted that the cliffside seemed smoother than the other more worn, ragged sections of the rockface. She remembered the Sunlight Tank and Midnight Zone required descending from the first floor and realized the whole section of cliffs under the lab must also be man-made or reinforced for it.

"Come along," the figure called out to Mel as she stopped to look at the lab. Mel turned back toward the others who were nearing the water and quickened her pace to catch up.

"Where's my sister?" Mel asked when she caught up. The longer they were with the figure, the less monstrous it seemed. Even though it walked through walls, had magic rope, and kept its face hidden, it seemed like a person to Mel.

The figure ignored her question and instead muttered to itself, "I should have just tied them up and carried them. They're seriously slowing me down." It stepped into the water and started wading out.

Mel grabbed Lewis's wrist to get his attention. "Where is it taking us?"

He shrugged. "Your guess is as good as mine. But it's toward where Sage is. And frankly, we have no other choice but to follow." He took off his shoes and socks and waded out after the figure.

Mel did the same but also noticed a few meters ahead of them that the water around the figure wasn't getting any deeper. It was now walking in water no higher than its shins. *That doesn't seem right... as you get farther away from shore, it should be getting deeper.*

"Follow exactly in a line behind me," it called back at them.

Mel realized her feet were no longer sinking into sand. Instead, they were on something solid. She glanced down at her feet and made out a metal strip about a meter wide that led out to the sea.

"Whoa!" Mel blurted.

"Yes, stick close. The bridge we're on is also retracting from the back as we walk, so if you don't want to end up swimming, catch up," the figure called out.

"What?" Mel and Lewis said in synchronized shock. They both ran until they were finally right behind the figure. When they'd caught up, the figure stopped. It picked up one of its feet and stomped down twice. The bridge below them started to rumble, and a metal mound broke the water's surface in front of them. Mel's mouth dropped in astonishment.

The figure stepped onto the mound, bent down, and opened a hatch. It motioned for Lewis and Mel to get inside. After they both got inside, the figure climbed in after them and closed the hatch.

"Welcome to my home." It pulled back its hood, revealing a wizened but handsome face of a lady in a tight bun with streaks of gray. "I'm Romilda."

CHAPTER 10

Before Mel could fully take in her surroundings, Sage dashed out from another room into her arms.

"Mel! You're here!" She buried her face into Mel's chest. Mel wrapped her arms around Sage tightly.

"You're human?" Lewis asked the now unhooded Romilda.

She laughed heartily. "Of course I am. What did you expect?" She turned around, exiting through a rounded doorway. "Come, this way."

Mel heard Lewis mutter to himself, "Humans who walk through walls. Humans who flicker and disappear. Different worlds? Don't blame me if I don't think this is normal."

Mel brought her face closer to Sage. "What happened? Did she kidnap you, too?"

Sage looked up and released Mel from her embrace. "Yeah. I was waiting for you both to lock up the lab. Suddenly, she grabbed me and covered my mouth, and I couldn't make any noise. She was super-fast and was carrying me down the cliffs when I freed my mouth and was able to call your name. But I don't think she realized you two were there with me until I called your name." She looked down at the floor. "Sorry, Mel. I got really scared."

Mel pulled her back in. "Don't be sorry. Sure, you got us also kidnapped by a mysterious lady." Sage gave Mel a side-eye from within the embrace. "But at least we're together. Seriously."

"Guys," Lewis said to them. "Look at this place."

Mel finally looked around and found they were in a nicely decorated foyer. It was round, with a large, ornate carpet in the center on which they were standing. A roaring electric fireplace crackled invitingly at one side with two armchairs across from it. Multiple openings scattered along the circumference of the room. Other than the piping and valves running along the metal walls, it felt like the inside of a quaint house. The opening Romilda just left through had white linen curtains hanging from the top.

The vessel they were in suddenly lurched as if coming alive from a deep slumber, jolting the trio out of their admiration of the room.

"Hurry on up, you three," Romilda called from the other room. They looked at each other, and Lewis broke eye contact first to start toward the curtained entrance after Romilda.

"Hold on," Sage said. She took Mel's hand, walked to Lewis, and took his hand in her other one. The three of them took a deep breath and walked through the curtain to find themselves in a kitchen. There was a large wooden table in the center with a bench and a stovetop to the left with a rounded brick hood above it. A sink was nestled in the tiled countertop, with various pots, pans, and spatulas hanging off the ceiling.

Sage whispered to Mel and Lewis, "I was in here the whole time. I tried looking for a secret compartment or something, but it's just a normal kitchen. I also couldn't get through that curtained entrance before. It was like it had an invisible barrier. It was only after I heard you all come back that I tried again."

Romilda was busying herself in the kitchen. She'd taken off her trench coat. Without it, Mel saw that she was a petite woman, a little shrunken by age, but still had great posture and seemed sprightly. She had a tea kettle going on the stove and a pot in which the contents were bubbling from the heat. She turned her head slightly to address them.

"Well, come in, will you? Don't just stand there. Come. Make yourselves useful." She turned toward the stove again, grabbed a ladle hanging above her, and took a sip of the pot's content. "The little one. Come, stir the pot."

Sage didn't dare argue and stepped around the large table to the stove.

Romilda sprinkled some ingredients into the pot and instructed Sage to keep stirring slowly. "Lewis, grab the cups from the cupboard." She pointed to the right side of the room with a large spoon.

Lewis wordlessly shuffled to the indicated cabinet to do as instructed. Romilda had taken the metal kettle off the stove and poured the hot water into another ceramic teapot. "I've already put the tea in here to steep. Pour some into each cup after a few minutes." She set the ceramic pot onto the table for Lewis.

"And you, umbrella girl." Romilda turned to Mel and smiled with her eyes wrinkling. Mel suddenly thought she looked vaguely familiar with that smile, confidence, and that tight bun. *Have I seen her before?* "Grab the spoons for the porridge." Romilda tapped a drawer at hip level with her large spoon. Mel forgot her thought and obliged.

The kitchen was bustling with movement. Everyone was busy with their tasks. The vessel itself was humming in movement as well. Romilda had Sage ladle scoops of porridge into bowls. The table was set with porridge, cups of tea, and utensils for everyone. They all sat with Lewis, Mel, and Sage on the bench at one side of the table facing the kitchen, and Romilda on the other side, facing them.

"Go ahead," Romilda prompted them to eat. "I'm sure you're all hungry."

Mel was hesitant. The bowl of rice porridge in front of her was steaming appetizingly, with bits of orange salmon flakes peeking through the generous garnish of green onions and minced ginger on top. Mel's stomach growled, but all three of them didn't make a move.

"I'm not going to poison you. I want to talk with you," Romilda addressed their inaction. She then took a large slurp of her porridge and a sip of tea. At that, Sage also took a bite of the porridge to Mel's dismay.

Seeing as Romilda was eating and drinking the contents from the same batch, Mel figured it was probably safe to eat. She took a tentative bite out of the porridge, and a warmth of savory carbs sprinkled with the richness of salmon spread from her mouth to her extremities. It was surprisingly good, and she inhaled one spoonful after the next. Lewis watched the two of them eating for a few minutes with a brow raised before he also picked up his spoon.

Once all three were busy with their steaming bowls of salmon porridge, Romilda stopped and watched them with a slight smile but neutral expression.

Lewis noticed first. "So," he started, "where are we? And why do you want to talk to us? Who are you?"

"This is my home," Romilda answered.

CHAPTER 11

"You live in a submarine?" The doubt was unmistakable in Lewis's voice.

"This is a submarine?" Sage interrupted between bites.

"Yeah," Lewis answered. "My mom works with submersibles. They're usually remotely operated or autonomous ones, which are smaller. She's brought me onto a few human-occupied ones, but none like this. This is... like a house."

"As expected of Dr. Trisham's son. You're right. This is one of a kind. I've lived on this submersible for almost thirty years."

"You know my mother?" Lewis asked.

"No, I'm referring to your father, Lewis. Dr. Carlisle Trisham."

Lewis looked stunned, and Mel remembered his father had disappeared when he was very young.

"I know he disappeared, Lewis. I'm sorry about that. I, too, was very shocked when I heard." Romilda softened her expression briefly. "But we don't have much time, and I'd like to get to that key around your neck, umbrella girl."

"Her name's Mel," Sage spoke up, and Mel smiled gratefully, but before she could try to deflect Romilda's question or ask for the reason Romilda was so interested, Sage continued. "It's a key our grandpa left behind. He died kind of young, but he left this for Mel. What's it to you?" It was like the food and having Mel and Lewis with her restored her courage and, unfortunately, recklessness. Mel pinched Sage's thigh from under the table. "Mel!" Sage protested at that.

Romilda had widened her eyes and gazed at the two of them in wonder. "Incredible," she uttered softly. "We never found him because... he stayed. He stayed there to keep the token safe."

"What do you mean? What do you mean by 'he stayed?' You said you knew the owner of this key. Did you know Grandpa?" Mel pushed.

Romilda shut her eyes and took a deep, shaky breath. "Now that I'm looking at you two," she made eye contact with Sage and Mel with a newfound warmth, "you *do* resemble Howler."

"Howler? Grandpa's name was Howard," Sage said.

Romilda smiled a smile that reached her eyes, and Mel once again felt she'd seen this woman before but couldn't place where.

"He changed his name, didn't he?" Lewis said to Romilda. "When he... went to their world?" He tilted his head toward Mel and Sage.

They both stopped eating and turned to Lewis in revelation. *Grandpa isn't from our town, much less our world? Could it be true Grandpa's from here? Is that why we don't know much about Grandpa's life before he met Grandma?*

"Your grandfather, who's from our world, and your father, Dr. Trisham," Romilda looked to Lewis, "were my good colleagues and incredibly intelligent. Some of the best engineers we've had."

"How was Grandpa an engineer if he didn't go to college?" Mel asked, "I thought he did carpentry trade school."

At that statement, Romilda guffawed heartily, slapping the table. "Howler? Not go to college? That's hilarious! He was one of the most accomplished dimensional mechanical engineers we've seen! No, no. He went to college and breezed through graduate studies. But on our stakeouts, he had always mentioned how he dreamed of opening a wood shop quietly." She paused in thought and added more gently, "I'm glad he got that opportunity."

"What's dimensional mechanical engineering, ma'am?" Lewis asked, interrupting Romilda's reflection. "I've never seen this as an option when researching high school specialties or university options." Mel, too, was curious about what that was.

"Ah, yes," Romilda snapped back and sat up straighter. "This field has since been rendered obsolete and deleted from all references. Let me start from the beginning."

Lewis, Mel, and Sage placed their utensils down and sat leaning slightly forward, listening with rapt attention to hear more about Grandpa and Lewis's father, people previously accepted to be a mystery in their lives.

Romilda got up to heat another pot of water in the metal kettle. "Many decades ago, when I was a little girl just about Sage's age, we had Intradimensional Envoys. This was a government job, and these were people who had the biological propensity to handle traveling intradimensionally."

"Don't you mean *inter-dimensionally*?" Sage asked.

Romilda gave her a funny look, prompting Mel to further explain.

"We umm… did a bit of research back home when we came here the first time the other day. On parallel or alternate universes."

"Interesting!" Romilda lightened as she came to sit back down. "So you were able to travel here once before already! You both truly are Howler's progeny." She beamed proudly. "No wonder the government has been in a tizzy as of late. Did you experience some nausea and dizziness?"

"Yeah! How did you know?" Sage chirped.

"It's normal for dimension traveling. And it's not inter-dimensional. It's *intra*. There is a world in the same dimension as ours—your world. Because it's in the same dimension, the time of day and concept of time is almost the same, and occurrences in each world affect the other. It's almost like they're overlapping one another, and we walk through our own worlds, unaware we're sharing the same space and molecules as another world. As such, we call these different worlds *layers* because they're like layers on the same dimension." She paused and looked at each of them to gauge their understanding, only to be met by empty stares. "Hold on. Let me grab something to help you understand."

She got up, opened a cabinet behind her, and pulled out a sheet of kitchen parchment paper and a sheet of aluminum foil. She sat back down and placed the two sheets in a stack, one on top of the other on the table. "Some say that humans cannot perceive both. Depending on where we are, we only perceive the 'top' layer." She put up air quotes when saying top. "Look here." She motioned for them to turn their attention to the sheets in her hands.

"We're only seeing the parchment paper because it's on top of the aluminum foil. That's the layer we perceive. But," she flipped the sheets so that the aluminum foil was facing them now, "if we travel to the other layer, we end up perceiving this one instead because it's the top one from our point of view. In actuality, these sheets should be overlaying within each other to be more accurate, but this is a simple explanation we give to our young Envoys."

Mel was still trying to wrap her mind around all of this, but in some way, it did make sense that depending on where they stood relative to the parchment paper and aluminum foil, they'd see one or the other. *How funny to see our worlds relegated to kitchen items.*

Romilda got up again to grab the tea kettle that was just about to whistle. After she poured each of them another cup of hot tea, she continued.

"Nausea is normal if you are in a layer you're not accustomed to perceiving. So, if you came from your layer to ours, you're now perceiving our layer as the top layer and that stresses your body, manifesting in nausea. Honestly, quite a mild reaction for dimension traveling. But because of that, when we discovered your layer and finally harnessed the science to travel freely, we engineered a drink that would help with the nausea. It's a simple electrolyte drink, so the government also decided to pilot it to the general public. It ended up being a huge hit and was purchased by a corporate company, but the GMA had the clever idea to engineer the portals between our layers as vending machines so that any Envoy would have the drink immediately at hand upon landing at their destination."

Mel thought about the slightly bubbly, clear drink she and Sage had consumed. "Would this drink happen to be something called Mensen?"

"That's right! I assume you ladies found it in the vending machine, then? Yes, Mensen engineering was for Envoys but still enjoyed by the public to this day." Romilda took a sip of her tea. "We only know of one other layer, which is yours." She nodded at Sage and Mel. "We call that the First Layer. The one that we're in right now is called the Second Layer. There was speculation at the time that there may be many more. But we could never figure out the formula for getting into any other layer. With this discovery and the harnessing of dimension travel, the GMA heavily advertised for young men and women to apply to be Envoys to communicate, foster relations, and trade with the First Layer. It was my dream job when I was a little girl. But not every person who applied could make it. We found only specific genetic traits allowed some to safely travel with mild side effects. And then others were prime candidates as they were completely immune to the effects of travel, like Howler."

"What do you mean?" Lewis asked.

"Early on, the government had some Envoys who were cream-of-the-crop students and researchers, as expected. But when they tried traveling via the vending portals, it either simply wouldn't work or... they'd go blind."

"What?" Mel and Sage exclaimed simultaneously.

Romilda shook her head sadly. "Scientists and engineers never quite figured out what went wrong to address it. They concluded that perhaps those people weren't suited for dimensional traveling, so when they tried, the body couldn't handle it and ended up unsure which layer to even perceive. Like they were stuck in-between. We had the best ophthalmologists attend to these blinded Envoys. But all the research and examinations showed nothing physically wrong with their eyes, yet all they saw was darkness. So, the only way to avoid this happening was to test for a biological propensity for travel. Simple genetic mapping to look for specific markers. But that was also only after they'd had enough of a sample size of people who had the proclivity for it to know which genetic markers to look for. Before then, we had hundreds spend years of their lives training, only to lose their sight. All for the cause." She took a long sip of her tea.

What's the cause? Mel pondered yet didn't want to interrupt the story.

A silence hung over the four of them before Lewis broke it. "But the government took care of them, right? The people blinded for this cause?"

"Hold on," Mel cut in. "Can someone please explain what the *cause* is?"

Lewis and Romilda responded automatically in a monotone together, "For the good of our society," as if it were a phrase sketched into their minds. Romilda then uttered a *tsk* in annoyed contempt and continued as if that answered the cacophony of questions running through Mel's mind.

"As for Lewis's question—the GMA claimed they were caring for them. We all thought they did, and I'm sure they did at first. By the time I was old enough, the genetic mapping was highly accurate, so I was ecstatic I was eligible. After which, I successfully tested into my Dimension Envoy license, which, may I add, was quite a fun test." Romilda slightly smiled at that. "But after I became an

Envoy and rose through the ranks, my mentor had me tag along on one of her tasks. She ended up driving us hours outside the city limits. I remember I asked her what sector we were going to, and she responded that we weren't going to a sector."

"Were you going to our world? The First Layer?" Sage ventured.

"No, by then, my mentor and I frequented the First Layer as it was within our purview. She instead took me to a dusty compound and told me we were delivering food and water to them per GMA mandate. I remember we arrived, unloaded the truck of food, and brought it in. Numerous senior citizens greeted us. It was like a retirement home, but with no attendants. As we put the food in their fridges, I realized all of them were blind."

Mel gasped. "You mean they were the older Envoys who weren't travel compatible?"

Romilda snapped her fingers and pointed at Mel in affirmation. "Yes. It was them. My mentor didn't say anything specifically, so I had to put two-and-two together. In retrospect, she may have been restricted from explicitly telling me about it. Now, at first, I thought it was amazing that our government would provide them a home, albeit a bit rundown, and that it continued to send them food and water, as GMA does with its Universal Food Care. But then I noticed, a lot of them weren't quite right in the mind."

"What do you mean?" Sage was engrossed in the story.

"They were all pretty peaceful. But some cowered in fear exclaiming how they couldn't see anymore. Some asked me if I knew who they were or when they could take their Envoy test. I realized, being this far out from the city, they didn't have access to Reminserum."

Lewis frowned. "That can't be right. All citizens have access to MAGMA facilities, free of cost," he recited. "Seeing as they sacrificed their vision, they must be well cared for."

"That's what I thought, as well." She turned to Lewis. "I didn't say much at first because we don't unnecessarily question our superiors. But I figured these senior citizens weren't experiencing varying states of dementia due to only old age. It was also expedited because they had no access to our Memory Rooms and serums."

Lewis furrowed his brows in doubt, but Romilda continued, "After we finished delivering the food and water to the blinded Envoys, my mentor drove us through the different sectors in our city. Specifically, through the neighborhoods of those who didn't have jobs or an income—those who the GMA claimed do not contribute to our society. I've driven through those neighborhoods before myself, and everyone seemed healthy. We hear statistics on how everyone is fed with a great quality of life. And I thought the same when my mentor drove us through. They looked like any other middle-class suburban neighborhood. But when I asked my mentor why she brought us through those areas, she merely told me to look more closely." She turned to Lewis. "Have you been to those neighborhoods?"

Lewis took a moment to remember before answering. "I have. There are none of those neighborhoods in my sector, but once, I wandered a bit farther than usual to another sector when skipping school." *As usual,* Mel thought disapprovingly. "They didn't particularly care

I was skipping school and didn't report it to enforcers. Everyone looked healthy, and there was a lot more activity in that neighborhood since no one goes to work. Or they have nontypical hours for their jobs."

"How about you visit that memory again, Lewis? You're young enough that it shouldn't be an issue, right?" Romilda had brought her elbows onto the table, interlocking her fingers while looking at Lewis with interest.

"Yes, I'm not at the age threshold yet," Lewis confirmed.

"Excellent." Romilda smiled. "Now, Lewis, think back to when you walked through that neighborhood. Examine it again."

He looked down in thought. Mel felt the need to hold her breath while he recalled a memory. She had been curious about what it was like for them, but to her disappointment, it just seemed like a normal person trying to remember something.

"Okay, I'm back at the neighborhood," Lewis said. "I'm walking through again. Smelling the sunshine, feeling the wind. Hearing that Pomeranian behind the fence bark. Gravel getting kicked up by my feet. People are just ignoring me."

"Look closely at those people. Tune in," Romilda prompted.

Lewis cocked his head slightly as if truly listening more intently. Mel and Sage found themselves leaning toward Lewis, hoping to catch some of these conversations within his memory somehow.

"A child is coming out from a house to my left across the street. Her eyes look... fraught with worry." He furrowed his brows at this discovery. "She's holding her mom's hand and telling her she needs to remember to feed her little brother. That it's not okay to keep forgetting him just because he's a newborn." His frown etched deeper. "Wait. I'm walking past these two adults sitting in front of a lawn to my right. They're conversing about how they're losing it and laughing, so I didn't think much of it then. But I can still hear their conversation as I walk past right now. The man is saying..." Lewis looked up from the ground to meet Romilda's gaze, "that he can't remember the last time he's been to a Memory Room. No pun intended. And that he and his wife are desperately trying to conceive so that they can have someone help with memory, but have been unsuccessful... and... he's afraid he'll eventually look at his wife and not recognize her."

Mel wasn't sure what to think.

"I see someone crying in their car with their windows down ahead of me."

"What're they crying about?" Romilda asked.

"She's distraught MAGMA wouldn't let her in. She says, 'I've tried so many times, but why won't they let me in? I just want to remember my mother's face once more. Just once more is all I ask' and she keeps asking 'why' in between her sobs."

Romilda nodded as she made her point. "You can keep looking through your memory if you'd like, but I think you see now, don't you?"

"How is this possible?" Lewis dissented. "There's at least one MAGMA in each sector! I saw it there! Why wouldn't they have access?"

Romilda sighed as if suddenly fatigued. "How many times do I have to tell you to look *carefully*?"

His face darkened in skepticism as he closed his eyes to better focus on the memory. "Fine, I'm looking. MAGMA is right there, at the end of the cul-de-sac. Why aren't they going there?"

"Keep approaching it," Romilda wearily instructed.

Lewis closed his eyes again. "Okay. I'm continuing toward it, and it looks completely—" He abruptly stopped.

"What?" Mel wished she could see it too.

"Completely... empty." He opened his eyes in frightful incredulity. "The doors are chained shut, and parts of it are crumbling."

Romilda sorrowfully looked at the ground. "Exactly."

"What does that mean, though?" Sage asked. "What does all of this mean? With the blinded Envoys and the unemployed not having access to MAGMA?"

"It's not just the unemployed, Sage," Romilda corrected her. "It's those who the GMA deems do not add value to society. It's those blinded Envoys who couldn't do much else, unemployed citizens, citizens with jobs that the government disapproves of, and the list continues. Those deteriorating Envoys have likely all passed by now, but the problem persists with others."

"What it means, Sage," Lewis started slowly after having seen with his own eyes via memory, "is that the government likely is using its power and oversight to restrict Reminserum and Memory Rooms from people. This way, they can control the population." Lewis regained his composure and looked at Romilda again, "But how has no one noticed this before and brought it to the Prime Minister's attention? Or to an enforcer? I'm sure if my mom knew about it, she'd report it to have this addressed! It seems to affect those in lower socioeconomic statuses greatly."

Romilda stood up and started gathering their emptied bowls and cups. "Those neighborhoods don't have an assigned enforcer. That's a resource the government won't spare for those they deem invaluable. As for why no one has noticed, think about it." She placed the dishes into the sink behind her. "The government has access to all of our memory recall. As long as they make sure we don't remember the unsavory bits, like the restriction of Reminserum, and have us remember the good deeds like Universal Food Care and enforcer community work, no one would remember. No one would know."

Romilda then walked toward the right side of the kitchen. Next to the cupboard was an entrance to another room. She beckoned for the three to follow her. Curious about the rest of this story and what else was within the submarine, they rose from the bench to accompany her.

As they trailed Romilda into the other room, Mel held Sage back to whisper to her. "Honestly, the Memory Room thing always seemed weird to me, but I just thought that's how it was here."

"I agree," Sage muttered back. "But I didn't know they were gatekeeping memory access from people! That's so scary. To slowly keep forgetting everything."

"Everything always on the tip of their tongue, but nothing they can do about it," Lewis interrupted from in front of them as he overheard. "At first, they lose periphery stuff and short-term memory. And eventually, they'll feel their core memories slipping. Until they forget those they love most. Until they lose themselves."

Mel remembered Mom's description of Grandpa with his dementia.

"Wait, Romilda," Mel called after her. The room they'd entered was divided into two sections. The half of the room closest to them was like a lab with tanks of marine life and equipment. One of the tanks had the snakelike ropes that Romilda used on Lewis earlier floating within it. Mel thought for a moment she saw eyes on one of them, but when she blinked, they were gone.

A computer screen connected to a control board of switches and gauges sat among the tanks as well. The second half of the room was a clear space with rounded glass, displaying the darkness of the water outside the submarine. Mel paused for a moment in wonder before continuing her thought. "Oh, uh, Romilda, if Grandpa was from the Second Layer, doesn't that mean he'd need access to MAGMA and Reminserum?"

Romilda situated herself in front of the computer screen and adjusted switches on the control pad. She looked at Mel. "Yes, he'd need to have regular access to these. Otherwise, he'd have progressively lost his memories without recall ability. Did Howler...?" Her voice broke a bit before she cleared it.

"Yeah, Grandpa was diagnosed with early-onset dementia. I hadn't realized the connection until just now." Mel's face fell.

Romilda nodded gravely and swallowed loudly. "I'm sorry to hear that. Your grandfather was one of the best and a dear friend." She paused, which was when Mel saw her strained neck and pursed trembling lips. "It's painful knowing such a wonderful mind went that way and that he chose that end to be with the beautiful family he built, like you two." Romilda's eyes were twinkling with suspended tears, but when she saw Mel looking attentively at her, she immediately collected herself. "We all carry a few vials of privately concocted memory serums on our person as backup, but it's hard to use without a Memory

Room. I'd imagine your grandfather decided to stay in the First Layer for many reasons, and as such, he was prepared to lose his memories."

Sage had wandered to the side of the room with a bulletin board of papers, pictures, and writing. Mel followed to hide her watering eyes from Lewis and Romilda. Her mother's saddened face at the thought of Grandpa and his failing memories had Mel welling up, but a picture on the bulletin board diverted her thoughts. The board had several photos of varying groups of people pinned up, but the one that caught Mel's attention was one she'd seen before. The very same photo inside Grandpa's photo album. She saw her grandfather standing at the side. It suddenly struck her that Romilda looked familiar because she was that handsome lady in the photo, with the tight bun, smiling confidently next to the seated people.

"Is that you in this picture?" She pointed at the lady in the photo.

Romilda looked up and grinned. "I guess I haven't aged too badly if you can still recognize me there. That's me about forty or so years ago."

Sage craned her neck to take a look as well. "The photo album Mom showed you when she handed you Grandpa's key?"

"Yeah, it's the same photo," Mel responded with wonder. She couldn't believe the lady in the photo was standing right here.

Lewis came over to take a look too. He shifted his focus to the other photos before exclaiming excitedly, "I... I think that's my father! I've seen so many photos of him at home. I think this is him!" He was pointing at another group photo. Mel took a closer look and saw

Romilda within it again, but this time, she was sitting at the front and had a few more wrinkles. She had the same confident smile, though.

"Indeed, that's Dr. Trisham, your father. All those photos are of teams I've led. Your father was on my team a few years after their grandfather. Dr. Trisham was pivotal in helping us stay hidden. After he disappeared, the GMA cracked our code and started flushing us out. I had to go into hiding and have been here ever since. I have all these photos and notes up to not only honor them but also to help me remember everyone as we've gone into hiding."

"Hiding?" Mel echoed. "If you were an Envoy, what do you mean they cracked your code and you had to hide?" She felt that Romilda wasn't telling them everything yet.

"Excellent question, Mel," Romilda acknowledged but remained tight-lipped as she tapped away on her computer.

Lewis nudged Mel to prompt her to ask again after Romilda's nonanswer, but she shook her head furiously. She didn't want to speak up again after being ignored. He glanced at Romilda across the room, deeply focused on whatever was on the computer screen, and decided she was distracted enough. He turned back to Mel and whispered to her and Sage, "Do you believe her? With the government controlling Reminserum access, controlling what people actually remember? I've never heard any of this, and my mom *works* for the government!"

"Yeah, but maybe your mom's memory is being controlled and limited by the government, too, right?" Sage whispered back. "Since she also uses their Memory Rooms, she probably doesn't know this is happening, like Romilda said."

"I don't know..." Lewis responded. "We've only just met her."

"But what reason would she have to lie to us?" Mel questioned.

"Well, for one. She wants that key around your neck, Mel. Maybe she's trying to convince us to hand it over nicely," Lewis pointed out.

Mel looked down at the key. "I'm pretty sure she could have taken Grandpa's key by force if she wanted to," she said quietly, remembering how easily Romilda overpowered them at Lewis's house.

Lewis also seemed to remember as he didn't have a rebuttal.

"I don't think she'd lie to us," Sage added. "She knew Grandpa and your dad. They were friends."

"We don't know that. The pictures just prove they were on her team," Lewis corrected her. "And even if she knew them and was friendly with them, that doesn't necessarily mean she won't lie to us just because we're their children. She basically kidnapped us, remember?"

Mel thought he did have a point. They shouldn't be so quick to trust everything Romilda said, but the fact was, she knew Grandpa. And given how other team members looked at her in those photos, Mel felt Romilda was trustworthy and principled. "Even if she is lying to us," Mel started, "I think the government control of memories could be true."

"How do you mean?" Lewis asked.

"Well, look at us." Mel gestured to herself and Sage. "We come from another world where we don't use Memory Rooms or Reminserum. Sure, our memories can be faulty and we make mistakes. But we have full control of our own memory recall. If we're from a place where everyone can be in control of their own memories, why can't it be that way here?"

Lewis frowned in thought. "You all don't have a photographic memory?"

"Some people do!" Sage added. "No one uses serums or special rooms, though."

Lewis contemplated some more. "Even though it's wild to me that there's a whole world of people walking around with potentially fuzzy memories, I suppose… it could be possible for people to have full authority over their own recall here. I always thought having the government do it was easier, but if they are restricting access and altering people's memories by merely not allowing them to recall certain things, then there could be other solutions to allow everyone their own control."

His qualms seemed dispelled for now, so Mel added, "Let's just see what more we can learn from Romilda. We can't really escape from this submarine if we wanted to, so I think being friendly with her is the safest bet right now."

Lewis nodded. "That makes sense. Maybe when she takes us out of the submarine, and we think things feel suspicious, we can make a run for it then. But it's a good idea to go with it for now. There is one question that's been burning on my mind, though."

"What is it?" Sage asked, but Lewis had turned to Romilda.

"This is a lot to take in, Romilda," he said. "And frankly, hard to believe. I know what you're saying is technically possible and logically makes sense. But, if you're also from my world—this second layer—how do *you* remember everything and can tell us all of this when you should need access to Memory Rooms as well?"

Romilda finally turned her eyes from the computer screen and looked at them. "I'm glad you asked, Lewis. I remember because I have a Memory Room. You're standing right in one."

CHAPTER 12

Mel surveyed the room they were standing in again. That's when she noticed the red creatures floating in the tank next to the computer and that the other half of the room, previously a clear glass showing the waters outside pressing on the submarine, was now a matte black, like a TV screen. Lewis also observed the red sea creatures next to Romilda.

"Are those... atolla jellyfish?" Lewis pointed at the tank. *Atolla jellyfish? Like the saucer-like ones at Lewis's mom's lab!*

Romilda tapped the tank. "That's right. This tank was outfitted to house them properly and extract their toxin to produce the serum. I'm not a biochemist, so I can't tell you how exactly it works. We had our scientists engineer a generic version of Reminserum and this entire submersible as a sustainable safehouse."

"So, you've been able to live here all this time?" Sage asked.

"Yes. Occasionally, I have to surface for some supplies, but I mostly stay at sea to stay off the grid."

"And you can capture atolla jellyfish yourself?" Lewis asked.

"That's right. This vessel can access the deep sea and set traps for the jellyfish. I have a dashboard here that notifies me if it's caught something, which is when I go down to retrieve it. This small tank that contains the atolla is also specially engineered to make the experience as seamless and nonstressful as possible. Lewis, your father worked on some of the engineering for this."

Lewis took another look around the room in awe as if he were stepping into it for the first time again.

"In fact," Romilda cleared her throat, "I brought you here to show you memories. It may be easier to show you rather than tell you."

"As in... you're going to recall and show us your memories?" Mel asked.

"Yes. This room is basically the same as any other MAGMA Memory Room. Just smaller. We retain all of our memories. We just have issues recalling them, as do people in the First Layer, like Mel and Sage. But we, in the Second Layer, have an exponentially worse problem with it, so we get a recall boost by injecting this jellyfish serum." Romilda patted a metal-coated syringe on her desk. She paused for a moment. "You know how you sometimes might have something on the tip of your tongue?"

Mel and Sage nodded.

"Well, Lewis never has that feeling because he's below the age threshold of development."

Mel and Sage looked at Lewis incredulously. He nodded solemnly, affirming he'd never had that issue.

"But, in your world," Romilda continued, "if anyone had that tip-of-tongue feeling, and you gave them a shot of this syringe, they'd instantly be able to remember what they were trying to remember. In this layer, we start having that issue at a serious level multiple times a day when we hit the age of eighteen. That's why we start using serums then. These are typically only in the hands of the GMA and administered at MAGMA, used in conjunction with Memory Rooms that display the memory onto huge screens, like a theater."

"But if you only need this serum to recall, then why do people need the Memory Rooms?" Sage asked.

"With Kanperetinentia plus memory recall issues," Lewis jumped in, "the serum just helps with us remembering what we wanted to remember. The Memory Rooms pick up that memory to help us extract and display it for us to look at. But if what Romilda says is true about the GMA controlling it, technically, they can intervene in that process. If they detect the memory requested to recall is something they don't want, they just don't display it and choose another closely associated memory to display."

"Hold on," Sage interjected. "You're saying the GMA can choose another memory to show you instead of the one you wanted?"

"Right," Lewis confirmed, "I've read my parents' notes. It has to be a closely associated memory to the one you're trying to recall, though. Otherwise, it'd be obvious it's not the one you wanted. If it's related, then you likely won't realize they're showing you something else."

"For example," Romilda tagged in, "if you're trying to remember where you had that delicious meal last week, but it's at a location the GMA doesn't want you to know exists, or you witnessed something at the restaurant they want to keep under wraps, they can pull another memory from last week during which you had a similarly satisfying feeling from eating another item."

That's insane… the government technically could control memories and people this way, through their own memories, Mel thought.

Romilda continued, "Well, time to answer some of your other questions. You were asking about why I'm hiding from the GMA." The trio nodded. "Go ahead and stand in front of the screen." She jabbed the syringe into her arm.

Lewis went ahead and stood in the space as instructed as he was familiar with Memory Rooms. He glanced back at Mel and Sage. "We just stand here and watch. Like a theater," he said to address their unease.

As Mel and Sage tentatively approached, the matte-black screen started swirling in gray.

"Here goes!" Romilda called from behind her control board.

***

A deeply disturbed, younger Romilda showed on screen before the rest of the environment formed on the large, curved display. Romilda sat in her cubicle with an elbow on her desk and a hand on her forehead. She was taking notes with the other hand. Mel took a step forward, and the screen automatically zoomed forward onto the note, giving her an extreme sense of vertigo.

"The floor you're standing on senses your movement. And based on your intentions, the screen reacts with my memory to bring you closer to things you're curious about or show you surroundings that aren't the current focus," Romilda explained.

"So, it's like an interactive screen?" Sage asked.

"I suppose that's another way to describe it, yes," Romilda responded. "Keep watching."

Mel turned back to the screen to see the note the younger Romilda was scrawling in perfect cursive.

Blinded Envoys, at-risk neighborhoods, no access to MAGMA.
<u>Propaganda?</u>

She'd heavily underlined the last word. The younger Romilda suddenly slammed her hand on the table and muttered under her breath, "It's no use! No matter how many notes I make to remind myself, I'll forget this if I'm using MAGMA. I'll soon forget this... am I... okay with forgetting this?"

She abruptly stood with gumption and ripped the notes she took out of the notebook. "I need to find Captain." She stormed off.

A swirl of gray once again filled the screen as the scene changed to the next memory. The younger Romilda was standing at the doorway of an office, facing another woman.

Mel turned her head slightly to look at the sign on the door, which displayed, Captain Norma Pilazzo. The young Romilda started speaking, so Mel turned her attention back to her.

"Captain, may I speak with you privately?"

The older lady at her desk looked up. "Sure, Romilda. You may close the door and come in."

The younger Romilda stayed where she was. "Perhaps, Captain, we may take a quick coffee break? I need to ask you for some... advice, as my mentor."

So Captain Pilazzo is the mentor who showed Romilda the blinded Envoys and those neighborhoods!

"We just had a one-on-one a few days ago, Romilda. Can this wait?" Captain Pilazzo had her eyes glued to the file in her hands.

"I'm afraid it can't, Captain. This won't take long."

Captain Pilazzo glanced at Romilda from over her glasses. With the young Romilda's look of determination and clenched fists, the Captain seemed to conclude it was important. "Well, everyone needs a break to recharge." She closed her file and stood up. "I know of a coffee shop nearby."

The gray smoke swirled across the screen again to show young Romilda and Captain Pilazzo facing each other inside a small coffee shop.

"I didn't know this place was here," young Romilda said as she looked around.

"It's easy to miss," the Captain responded. "But I come here when I want to speak privately and... don't want to be heard."

Young Romilda looked at the Captain in bewilderment. "How did you know I wanted to talk about sensitive matters?"

"When you suggested we go out instead of speak inside my office, I deduced it's something you don't want others at work to hear."

Pilazzo noticed young Romilda glancing at the coffee shop owner, who was wiping down mugs with a cloth. "You don't have to worry about him. Now, tell me to what do I owe this pleasure, Romilda?"

Young Romilda took one more wavering glance at the coffee shop owner before turning back to the Captain. "I wanted to talk about what you showed me the other day—delivering food to the blinded Envoys and those neighborhoods. I've been trying to hold onto these memories before I lose them, and it's only a matter of days. I had to talk to you now because I know I won't remember again if I need to use MAGMA's Memory Rooms."

"How do you mean?" the Captain took a sip of her coffee with what looked like a knowing smile to Mel.

"If no one is aware of the GMA restricting access to Reminserum, and we all thought everyone was happy, I figured the only way to keep this sealed is because the government doesn't let us recall any memories of that if we encounter it. It's the only thing that makes sense, especially since the GMA is the only entity with access to the resources for these memory serums and the technology for the rooms. So before I fully forget, I need to ask you, Captain, why? Why did you bring me that day? And then why did you not say anything else? Why did you show me these things?" Young Romilda was worked up with these questions.

Captain Pilazzo sat silently, warming both her hands on her coffee mug. Mel could see where Romilda possibly picked up the habit of not responding to questions immediately.

At no response, young Romilda tried again, "Captain, I need to—"

"I'm glad you came to me," Pilazzo finally said. "I've observed you for many years as you've grown. I determined you're able to think logically and differentiate between right and wrong. You consider all the facts before acting, and you act in the interest of the whole. You have a bright future ahead of you here with GMA and among Envoys. And these are exactly the reasons I decided to show you these things the other day." She took a sip. "And the fact you came to me means I made the right decision."

Young Romilda had one brow lifted quizzically, so Pilazzo continued.

"The fact you came to me to ask about it after I showed you means you're bothered by what you saw." The Captain looked at young Romilda again from above her glasses. "If you were indifferent, you would have been fine with forgetting it, and we wouldn't be sitting here right now."

Young Romilda steeled herself. "You're right. It's been driving me nuts. It's shattered my very image of our government. I dedicated my life to it, only to see this? The GMA abusing its power and the trust our people have in it? I'm not okay with forgetting. But I also can't understand why you'd show me these things when we can't do anything about it."

"That's where you're wrong, Romilda." Pilazzo leaned back in her chair. "I'll tell you straight up and give you a few seconds to express shock but control it as I need you thinking clearly."

"What?" Young Romilda was already alarmed at that disclaimer.

"I'm part of an underground society called The Mastodons."

"Mastodons? As in the extinct mammoth?"

"Yes. We're named after those distant relatives of the elephant as they're known to have long memories. About a decade ago, our founders realized the GMA was not providing accessible Memory Rooms to all populations, as they've always touted. They realized this when there were some discrepancies in historical accounts as one of them was a highly decorated history professor and researcher. He discovered after the perfection of Reminserum and the scientific improvements to harness this, the government started controlling what people remembered. Over time, that can result in changed historical accounts, even deleted history simply because it's forgotten."

Mel took a look at the young Romilda and saw the usually put-together woman was slack-jawed.

"It's said," the Captain continued, "when this history professor noticed these discrepancies, he brought it to a few colleagues, but no one listened. He had the sense to realize there may be something more afoot, so he kept his mouth shut and continued digging. He happened to have a childhood friend who worked as a biochemist at the GMA who was also uneasy about how closely guarded Reminserum and the engineering of Memory Rooms are. They founded the Mastodons. A society of people dedicated to ensuring accurate historical accounts of our nation and world, and toward the realization of an equal society where all people have equal access to our own memories."

Young Romilda's mouth was now fully open in shock.

"When the government harnessed the ability to travel to the First Layer and found people who don't need memory serums—people who don't spiral into dementia—the Mastodons thought this was our chance. By showing our citizens there are worlds out there of people who have full access to their own memories, maybe we can pressure the GMA to stop safeguarding its technology. And perhaps, by opening these portals to the public, people from both layers can freely walk between the two, and as people from both layers start creating families together, perhaps in the future, we'd have people who simply no longer need Reminserum."

"But that didn't happen," young Romilda said. "Only those with the propensity for traveling intradimensionally can safely transport."

Captain Pilazzo looked down in disappointment at that. "You're right. The fact that only a select few of the population could travel without major side effects was a hurdle in our plans. Regardless, this realization of our people seeing how others live without serums can still help. Perhaps our Envoys will start families, and we can have a few people living in the First Layer should they choose. Our plan would take longer, but it could still work."

"What did the Mastodons do?"

"We started installing our own people into the GMA's Envoy program. I'm one of the first. And then we waited for time to do its work. However, we didn't realize the government would also put a tight lid on our discoveries in the First Layer. The existence of another world and the Envoy program were common knowledge when I was younger. But we realized an increasing number of common citizens didn't even know we had an Envoy program, much less that another world exists. As Envoys, we had to sign a contract that we wouldn't share information about what we've seen or what we're working on. But we realized that even when mentioned casually with friends at dinner tables, more and more were returning with blank stares. I think your cohort of Envoys has noticed this."

"An increasing number of my friends have no idea what I do. They think I'm doing some sort of virtual reality government work," young Romilda agreed.

"It's been a long process for the GMA," Captain Pilazzo said. "But they're best at the long game, and they're definitely slowly removing the knowledge that another world exists by making sure no one remembers. As a result, our occupation as Envoys is being forgotten as well. Anyone who may realize this or opposes this will soon forget and no longer be an issue for the GMA."

"How do you remember, Captain? How do the Mastodons remember?" young Romilda asked.

At that, the Captain smiled. "Because that founder who's a biochemist? He was able to replicate Reminserum and steal the plans for building a Memory Room."

"He what!"

"Of course, to be able to function independently from the government, we need our own access to serums and Memory Rooms. We can't risk using MAGMA. With that founder's knowledge and the stolen plans, the Mastodons were able to create Memory Rooms for our own usage and work toward our goal."

"Are you implying there are Memory Rooms not at MAGMA?" Romilda asked incredulously.

"I'm not implying, Romilda. I'm saying there are. This coffee shop is one of our locations. The owner here, Volam, is from one of the founder's family." Young Romilda looked at the innocuous man still wiping down his mugs and espresso machine. "He altered memory serums into a digestible form, and so, he adds a few drops into our coffee whenever a Mastodon member stops by to help us hold over."

The man named Volam looked up and nodded his head slightly before continuing to clean his station.

"Is this a massive network?" Romilda leaned forward. "A digestible memory serum? Just imagine what the government would say if they caught wind of this! Everyone could easily have some to drink!"

"It's not as strong as the injectable memory serums, but it helps over time. However, because it's not as potent, it's not feasible for everyone to only drink this for their memories. And our facilities aren't large enough to create this for the public," Captain Pilazzo answered.

"How many Mastodons are in the GMA? How many are Envoys? How do you hide the fact you're a Mastodon from the GMA when you work for them too?"

"We don't have many because it requires extreme control to make sure we're not even remotely thinking about the Mastodons when we use a MAGMA Memory Room. Otherwise, they can search our associated memories to find it. It's not easy not to think about something that means so much to us. When deciding who we can place at GMA positions and who we can even take into our numbers, potential candidates go through our Memory Room test to determine whether they can hide their thoughts on the Mastodons."

"That's incredible," young Romilda said, "and I can see why that limits the Mastodon's numbers."

"That's why I showed all those things to you, Romilda. We can only take in the best of the best. You're one of the best with the potential to rise in the ranks at the GMA."

Romilda looked up. "You're... recruiting me?"

Volam strode over to top off their coffees.

"I was recruiting you when I first showed you the blinded Envoys," Captain Pilazzo said with a grin. "Your declining my invite would be if you never came to me to talk about it."

"Wait, wait, wait," young Romilda said quickly. "I haven't agreed yet. You're asking me to betray my country. This is treason."

"I'm not asking you to betray your country. The Mastodons stand for our people. I'm asking you to join us in overturning a power-hungry, controlling government and saving our people from being merely sheep. Pull everyone out of the darkness. The GMA doesn't have the people's best interest at heart. It's been slowly deleting and altering history—it's controlling people through their memories. I'm asking you to help right this. It wasn't always like this."

"What do you mean that it wasn't always like this?" young Romilda asked.

Captain Pilazzo checked her watch. "Our time is up. We need to return to the office, but come to me again in a few days, and I'll explain."

"What if I forget?"

"Volam gave you a few drops of memory serum in your coffee today. That should hold you out for another week or so. We'll meet again in a few days at this coffee shop during your lunch break. I expect you to have an answer on joining the Mastodons then, as well." The Captain got up and pulled out a few coins for Volam to pay for the coffee.

"Which day will we meet here again?" Romilda asked.

"All I can say is within the week. I'll signal you on the day of. Now, no more of this talk. Today, we discussed how you can do better at your job and the path toward a promotion as far as anyone knows."

The screen covered in gray smoke again, ending the memory.

CHAPTER 13

At the end of the series of memories Romilda showed them on her submarine, the trio simultaneously exploded with questions.

"So *did* you join the Mastodons?" asked Sage.

"A memory serum that we can ingest? How has the GMA not even thought of this?" Lewis asked at the same time.

"Deletion of history? Through people's memories? What about written firsthand accounts?" Mel inquired.

"Slow down, all right!" Romilda spoke above their voices to quiet them down. "Many times in history, people document events after the fact. It's easy enough for the government to restrict memories of what's written in that case. For accounts recorded in real-time, it's also easy enough for the GMA to track these accounts down and make sure they never meet the public eye. Now for Lewis's question, perhaps the government has thought of it, but they never explored it as it would make serums more accessible, which is exactly what they don't want. And Sage, hold tight. This next memory will answer your question." She clicked away at her computer and stabbed another syringe into her arm.

The three of them turned their attention back to the large screen, waiting for the gray swirls to clear.

An image materialized of young Romilda and Captain Pilazzo sitting at the same coffee shop but at a different table this time.

"I'm glad you caught my signal to meet today," Captain Pilazzo said to young Romilda.

"The usual?" Volam asked the Captain.

"Yes. And you, Romilda?"

"I'll have it black," young Romilda said.

Volam nodded in acknowledgment and went back to his station.

Young Romilda turned to the Captain. "You said last time that it wasn't always like this. What did you mean by that? Do you mean that the government wasn't always controlling memory access?"

Captain Pilazzo turned away to watch Volam make the coffee. "It started when the Bellows family came into power."

"Bellows? The family of the last fifteen prime ministers? They're adored by the people!"

"Indeed. They're well-loved by our people. And for good reason, like executing the initiative to unarm our enforcers and change their role from fear-mongering officers to officers the community can count on. They've done a great many things to improve our society. And it probably helps that all the Bellows prime ministers have been strikingly handsome."

Lewis interjected, "Oh, yes, you can practically find Prime Minister Gio Bellows's picture in every magazine. I'm pretty sure my sister has a crush on him." He rolled his eyes.

"Shhh!" Mel and Sage hushed him.

"So what about the Bellows family?" young Romilda asked Pilazzo.

"Do you remember our previous prime minister, Romilda?"

Young Romilda scrunched her face pensively before responding, "No, I don't remember his face exactly. I just remember he was also relatively handsome. Although his hair was gray, he aged pretty well."

"Exactly," Captain Pilazzo said as Volam placed their coffees in front of them. "No one remembers any of the previous prime ministers' faces clearly. And if we try to look them up, photos of them don't exist. They've been removed or deleted. As for printed media, the data retention law for printed materials is about five years in most places, so most institutions have trashed old photos. The government does audits on media companies each year, saying they're ensuring honest reporting but also to remove anything that's too aged. The GMA also sends cleaning companies to every household yearly, claiming they're helping our citizens declutter as a free service, but it's actually to remove anything too old. Any old pictures of the Bellows family that anyone could have cut out or hung up or have lying around in their restrooms as toilet reading—all that is removed."

"I've never thought twice about the cleaning service," Romilda said in an astonished voice. "I've always appreciated it because it saves me time when getting rid of old furniture and items. But why does it matter that they're throwing away old things or photos of previous prime ministers?"

"That's because the lineage of Bellows prime ministers has actually been... the same man."

"What!" Young Romilda leaped to her feet with both hands gripping the table's edge. Some of their coffee spilled into the saucers from the sudden agitation.

"Control your emotions, Romilda." The Captain calmly wiped her saucer. "Regardless that Volam's coffee shop is one of the Mastodon's locations, it's still a public coffee shop."

Two men had entered the shop in a rush with their briefcases at that moment, their entrance announced by the tinkling bells hung above the doorway.

"How may I help you today?" Volam greeted them.

One of the men gave young Romilda, who was still standing and clenching the edge of the table, a funny look.

"Look," the Captain proclaimed loudly enough for the men to hear. "Just because you're working hard doesn't necessarily mean you'll get a promotion immediately. Morgan got the promotion this time, and there's nothing you can do about it."

Young Romilda turned back to the Captain before it registered on her face. "I'm sorry. I got frustrated my contributions weren't noticed," Romilda played along.

Mel looked back at the two men, and they seemed unbothered by young Romilda now and were back to their own riveting discussion while ordering coffee. After they left and the door shut behind them, Romilda spoke again in a hushed voice.

"The same man has been our prime minister all this time? You're talking decades! The Bellows family started even before we were both born. It's been the same family, but the position has passed from father to son each generation. How could it be the same man?"

Pilazzo sighed, and Mel thought she suddenly looked very exhausted. "We're not entirely sure how it's possible. The Mastodons found out by accident, and through some investigations, sure enough, it's been the same man for decades. Aging, and then coming back in his prime. That much, we can confirm. There have been reports from our undercover agents that his family, a family of scientists, discovered the formula for the elixir of youth, but it's unconfirmed. None of our people can get close enough."

"Isn't the elixir of youth a myth?" Romilda's voice was laced with doubt.

"That's what they tell us to think. But I've found that many myths may have a drop of truth. Given our research on genetics when it came to the Envoy propensity for intradimensional travel and our research on memories, what's to say there's no research on cell biology to live forever? Or it could be clones with memory transfer to a new body." The Captain shrugged as if she were talking about everyday matters like the weather. "Anything's possible."

Young Romilda was at a loss for words, so Pilazzo took a few sips of her steaming coffee. "The facts are one: it's been the same man as prime minister, and two: memory access control started during the Bellows's reign. Seeing as he seems to live forever, or at least, have a very long lifespan, he has plenty of time to slowly gain more power without any uprisings because all this is happening on a micro-level across generations. I'm not recruiting you to the Mastodons to fight the government. I'm asking you to help us in this fight to bring down a man who's been the root of our problems. I need to know your answer. Will you fight with us or turn a blind eye?"

Young Romilda didn't immediately respond. When she finally raised her head to meet the Captain's eyes, she asked, "Why are you trying to recruit me?"

The Captain looked slightly exasperated. "I told you the other day it's not easy for us to recruit because we need to be able to keep memories of the Mastodons away from the GMA when using MAGMA Memory Rooms. I determined you can do that. But also, we received reports the GMA is shutting down our vending portals to the First Layer."

"What!" Young Romilda jumped to her feet again.

"Romilda! What did I say earlier?"

Romilda sat back down. "I'm sorry, what?" she asked more softly. "When will they shut us down?"

"It's unclear. The GMA will likely transfer Envoys to other branches, and we'll all eventually forget what exactly we were doing before. It's now paramount for us to keep portals open. If we were to close these, we'd be taking a step backward in our development as a society. When we discovered the people in the First Layer without the need for memory aids, this threatened the Prime Minister's rule, so he's finally making a move. If people knew of another world where humans don't need the government's help, pockets of academics would start questioning the GMA and lead to dissatisfaction among the people. But what we don't know, we won't know is possible. If we don't know about the people in this other world, then our world is the only thing we know of. And to us, the GMA works for the good of our society—the Bellows can do no wrong."

Young Romilda now had her head between both hands.

"We need more talent," the Captain continued, "and you have the leadership capabilities and quick thinking we need. On the other end, we're working on recruiting more engineers and undercover agents. If there's nothing we can do about the government closing portals, then we need to create our own."

"Create our own vending portals?" Young Romilda looked up.

"Correct. Once everything closes, I'll bet the prime minister will either burn all previous research or lock it up within his manor. We need to get the research somehow or plans to create these portals on our own."

"That's easier said than done," Romilda responded, sitting straight again. "The engineering of these vending machines into portals is difficult enough. But you also need to create the blue power stones to run them. On top of that, there's the engineering of Mensen to address side effects of traveling."

"We've already gotten our hands on the Mensen recipe. One of our members, fortunately, is head of a beverage conglomerate and partnered with the government to produce the drink, so we got that. But the other two pieces are more difficult. We're aware of that and the seemingly impossible task in front of us, but although our numbers are few, our reach is wide and extremely talented. I'll ask you once more, Romilda, will you join us? Are you okay with the prime minister's antics? With forgetting all of this and living back in the shadows after a taste of the light?"

"Captain," Romilda crossed her arms playfully, "the way you ask is kind of leading, isn't it?"

Captain Pilazzo smiled, and Romilda continued, "But you also already knew my answer, didn't you?"

CHAPTER 14

"You were recruited by your previous mentor into their society to keep the portals active because the government shut down the whole program?" Sage exclaimed as the screen went back to matte black.

Romilda stood up from her computer. "Yes. As a Mastodon, we dedicate ourselves to maintaining the freedom and potential of intradimensional travel because it can lead to the freedom of our people to have full rights to their own memories. The Prime Minister shut everything down so our people wouldn't know there are other options out there. Places like your world where you can access your own memories."

"And the Prime Minister has been... the same person for decades?" Lewis was stunned. "That's not possible! Prime ministers are only allowed two terms maximum."

"I know it's hard to digest, Lewis. Our Prime Minister has done great campaigns and marketing. But by limiting access to memories, he started to abuse his power and use it for his own gain. He made sure we didn't remember his face across decades. All the rhetoric that it's been an honorable position passed down by his family is false. It's all been him." Romilda picked up one of the emptied syringes that previously held memory serum and jabbed it into a slot next to the atolla jellyfish tank to refill. "It was by chance that we found out."

"I need to sit down." Lewis walked to a chair next to the bulletin board.

"Take a moment, but I'm about to recall another memory for you. I came looking for you because of that key around your neck, Mel."

Mel instinctively brought her hand up to touch it.

"That key is what we call a *token*. Envoys each have one. It's like an identifier, so portals will register who last used it. It also saves the last traveled location within it, so you can always find home or where you came from. We stopped using our tokens long ago because the GMA hacked our systems. So when yours went live, I got a notification on this submarine. I recognized your grandfather's token and knew I had to get to you soon because the GMA will be getting the same ping."

"Wait a moment. My mom said the government was alarmed by something and everything's a mess right now, but that was when Mel and Sage first traveled without their grandfather's token. So the government wouldn't have gotten a notification then," Lewis said from his chair.

"The vending portal Mel and Sage traveled through on the First Layer is an unregistered machine. It's a vending portal the Mastodons created. But the portal in the Second Layer they arrived through *is* a government machine. As such, the GMA likely received a notification their machine went live, but seeing as these vending machines are often used for civilian consumption, it could have been a false alarm. But the Prime Minister is very careful, so it makes sense that when they got that first notification, although they weren't sure, they got in a tizzy," Romilda explained.

"So, when we came back with Grandpa's token, that's when they definitively knew that someone was traveling?"

"That's right. And that confirms my fear the government knows someone who doesn't belong is here," Romilda agreed. "I knew I had to get to you before the GMA did. Fortunately, the government's system isn't able to pinpoint the location of our tokens as accurately as our own systems, so I was able to find you first. It was particularly important to not let Howler's token fall into the GMA's hands."

"Why's that?" Sage ventured.

"Your grandfather's token has another functionality that he built into it—something we need to continue creating the power stones that run these portals. Howler was a lead engineer in replicating the stones, and miraculously, he succeeded. We had another engineer piece together a new vending portal and disguise it as a snack machine instead of a beverage machine as it usually is."

"The very machine in our town!" Sage said excitedly.

"That's right. We had to rush our plans to install it there because the GMA had already removed most of the vending portals from the First Layer then. Without an existing GMA portal, we wouldn't even be able to get to the First Layer in the first place to install our own disguised one. But it was a race against time because once we used their machine, they'd receive a notification of unauthorized use—we had to time how long it'd take the GMA to react to us and deploy their specially trained enforcers. But if we could get our Mastodon portal installed successfully, it would ensure we had one last portal there once the GMA closed the program, and we could continue our plans from there."

"Why did you need to use the GMA portal to get there first?" Mel had gotten a bit lost in the story.

"Our engineers couldn't figure out how to open new portals as the government did when they first harnessed this ability to travel. Our people could only reverse engineer vending portals. Basically, we didn't know how to program our machine to connect to a layer with zero existing portals."

"So why is Grandpa's token so important?" Mel asked.

"Howler replicated the power stone in theory, so the first time he actually created one was for the Mastodon vending portal. Because we were short on time, we couldn't properly test the stone, but Howler was confident. Seeing as he's the only one who knew how to make it, and we had to safely guard how he did it, right before the mission to install the machine, he told us that should anything happen, the key to replicating his work was within his token."

"What happened to the mission?" Sage demanded. "It succeeded, right?"

"I was leading the mission that night, and Howler was on my team. He was delivering the power stone, and I was bringing the vending portal. We have shrinking technology, so, fortunately, it wasn't difficult to lug around a giant machine."

Mel looked at Sage to see her mouth, "They have shrinking technology!" Mel shrugged in response. *Seems like anything is possible in the Second Layer.*

"But the Prime Minister responded more quickly than we expected," Romilda continued. "Howler and I met, but his stone was being temperamental. I decided to act as the distraction and drew the enforcers away from the machine and Howler as he tried to solve the issue. I managed to lose them and come back to the Second Layer, but that was the last I saw of Howler. None of us knew what happened to him, and we thought his token was lost. Throughout these years, no one's come close to replicating the power stones. And when the GMA cracked our token codes soon after Lewis's father disappeared, we thought all hope was lost and went into hiding. That's why I've been here." Romilda motioned to the submarine. "Forty years of guilt later, I finally have my answer to where your grandfather was. I don't know what happened with him that night, but something likely prevented him from coming back, so he stayed to keep his token out of the Prime Minister's hands." She looked at Mel and Sage again with a look of longing. "And he stayed for his new life."

All four of them were silent for a bit before Romilda started typing at her computer again. "I'm pulling a memory of the item we suspect Howler's key opens. In fact, Lewis, your father was the one who found the item," she added with a wink.

Mel saw Lewis's eyes light up as they walked back to the center of the room. She turned her attention to the screen swirling in gray again.

There was a young man who looked uncannily similar to Lewis and just like the man in the photos at their house. Mel glanced at Lewis peripherally and could see his eyes were as wide as saucers, staring at the screen.

"Romilda!" the man exclaimed. "You won't believe what I found while I was doing inventory."

This Romilda was still younger than the Romilda who sat behind the computer screen right now, but she had a few more wrinkles on her forehead and around her eyes than the Romilda they saw with Captain Pilazzo. "What is it, Carlisle?" she asked while looking at a city map with dots scattered throughout.

"I think I found something that belongs to Howler."

"Oh, great. Add that to the many things we've found," this Romilda responded sarcastically.

"No, this one's different. It's locked. And none of his keys fit. Remember you told me about his token and how it holds his research for replicating power stones?" Carlisle said frantically.

"Sure, but that's a lost cause, Carlisle. I'm trying to concentrate here."

"Yes, the key is lost, but what if this is the item his token opens? What if this has his research?"

The younger Romilda turned to face Carlisle. "Show me."

Carlisle immediately cleared the table in front of them and ran into the other room. He came back and set a small metal box on the table. It was about a foot in length and width with a locked padlock at the front.

"Wait a second. I've seen that box before!" Lewis whispered excitedly.

Romilda, on the screen, had rolled a chair over, sat down, and took the box into her hands. "You say all of Howler's other keys don't fit?" she said to Carlisle as she pulled on the lock.

"That's correct."

Romilda turned it over and looked at an inscription on the bottom. "This is undeniably Howler's. It has his token number on it."

"Well?" Carlisle asked.

"Let's break it open," Romilda gave the order.

"Yes! I was waiting for you to say that." Carlisle brought out a lock pick and a hammer, and a swirl of gray smoke filled the screen to end the memory.

Lewis looked to Mel and Sage. "I've seen that box before! I know exactly where it is!"

"And that's why I need your help," Romilda had left the computer and pulled up a chair to sit closer to them.

"When Lewis's father, Dr. Carlisle Trisham, joined us, he found a box he thought could be what Howler's key opens. It had Howler's token number on it, and none of Howler's other keys fit in the lock. We then tried to break the lock by force but couldn't. We think Howler fortified it somehow. It was one of Carlisle's projects to examine it to force it open. As such, I figured it would be in his office, correct?" She looked to Lewis, and he nodded. "I know Carlisle kept a lot of devices and books, and I saw no reason to retrieve it, but now that we have Howler's token, my immediate plan was to procure his box inside Carlisle's office. Seeing as you know exactly where it is in his office, you can easily go in and grab it."

"You mean we could potentially open the box?" Mel asked.

"Yes, now that we have both the token and box," Romilda said while checking her watch. "We don't have long, I presume. It's only a matter of time before the Prime Minister's people track you to Lewis's house. They'll likely enter and potentially grab the box if they realize Howler's token number is on it. Can I trust you, Lewis, to grab the box and bring it back before it falls into the Prime Minister's hands?"

Lewis hesitated with his previous uncertainty about Romilda, but seeing his father working with younger Romilda seemed to appease his doubts about her.

Romilda noticed and added, "If I meant badly, I could have taken Howler's key and determined the box's location through your memories, Lewis. It's easy enough for us to connect you to the Memory Room and prompt memories of the box through questions to extract information. But, I think having your help and having you all on board is important. I cared for your father and their grandfather, and they dedicated their lives to this."

Lewis thought for a moment before turning to Mel and Sage. "What do you think?"

"I believe her," Sage immediately responded. "With everything she showed us in her memories—and our grandpa worked with her. I think we need to help."

Lewis looked to Mel for her thoughts.

"I think it's worth a shot to see what's in the box. But I'm coming with you," Mel finally said.

"If Mel's going, I'm going, too!" Sage added with gumption.

Lewis mulled over their input quickly before turning to Romilda. "I'll do it. I'll grab the box, but it's all three of us. You can't keep one of us here just to get us to come back."

Romilda laughed. "Wouldn't even think to do that. I trust you'll all be back. I'll resurface the submarine and erect the walkway to shore. You'll have to move quickly. We've spent much too long explaining everything. Get back to the room with the main hatch." She rushed off.

"I remember the way." Lewis sprinted toward a doorway among the multiple openings of the room. Mel grabbed Sage's hand and ran after him. As they ran past the kitchen, she could feel the submarine moving. They got to the first circular room with the fireplace. Romilda's voice boomed over an announcement system.

"Grab the box and come back to shore. I'll be here waiting. If you run into trouble, I'll be near. Go now, and remember, you have limited time before the Prime Minister's people could be at your doorstep." The opening at the top of the room suddenly popped open, and Mel could see the blue skies beyond.

"After me," Lewis said as he started climbing the ladder up toward the opening.

CHAPTER 15

The three emerged from the submarine, ran along the partially submerged metal bridge back to shore, and climbed up the stairs along the cliff. Lewis led the way back to his house, with Mel and Sage in tow. Although Mel's lungs were starting to burn, she felt much more clearheaded breathing the fresh breeze rather than the recycled air within Romilda's place.

"We've decided to trust Romilda for now?" Sage hollered above the sounds of the coastal wind and their hurried steps.

"This is our only chance to run away if we want to," Mel said between breaths.

"Yeah, let's go with her plan for now!" Lewis yelled back. "She knows where I live anyway, and you don't know if you can get back to the First Layer either."

At that, Mel realized they could have asked Romilda how to use Grandpa's key to return properly, and they'd missed their chance. Every time they'd traveled had happened by mere luck. She silently berated herself.

"Plus," Lewis turned his head slightly to the side to throw them a mischievous look, "aren't you curious if your grandfather's key will open the box?"

***

They'd arrived back at Lewis's house with his mom's looming lab behind it.

Lewis checked his watch. "No one should be home yet. Mom should be at MAGMA, and school isn't out yet, so my sister shouldn't be here either."

They entered his house through the front, and as Lewis closed the door, a voice came from inside.

"Is that you, Mom?" Lewis's sister, Cartier, stood in the kitchen with her head peeking out from behind the open fridge door. "Oh!" She directed at Lewis once she saw him. "It's just you." Then she looked at the other two at the doorway, frozen in shock, "Hey, Mel. Hey, Sage." Mel was surprised Cartier remembered them since she had only met her once before.

Sage had the same thought as she blurted out, "You remember our names?"

"Yeah, of course, I do. I just met you both the other day," Cartier retorted, seemingly offended. "Why wouldn't I remember you? It's not like I'm eighteen yet." She grabbed an apple sauce out of the fridge.

"Oh, hey, Cartier," Lewis stuttered quickly, trying to mask his initial surprise. "Shouldn't you be at school? Or doing some class president things you do?"

"Yes, but it's lunchtime." She rolled her eyes as she shut the fridge. "We eat lunch at home today, remember? We do this once a week with Mom, where we all come back for a quick meal?"

"Oh, it's that day of the week?"

"Are you forgetting things already?" Cartier smirked.

"I didn't forget! I just lost track of the days," Lewis defended himself. "With your age, you're the one who'll be needing a Memory Room soon!" He turned to Mel and Sage while looking annoyed. "That's how kids make fun of each other here. We joke that they're already losing their photographic memory before age eighteen."

Cartier raised both brows. "Why're you explaining that to them? Kind of a weird statement."

Mel realized they were potentially making Cartier suspicious with their questions and Lewis explaining how things work. *But there's no way she'd even suspect we're from another world.* For good measure, though, Mel added, "Yeah, Lewis, we get it. What a weird thing to say!" She nervously laughed.

"Anyway." Cartier turned back to the yellow booklet in her hands. *It's the Prime Minister's book!* "Mom should be home soon with lunch, but if your friends are joining us, you need to call her to let her know." Cartier plopped herself on a kitchen island bar stool and intently flipped to a page of the booklet to peruse.

"They won't be joining for lunch!" Lewis immediately said. "Actually, I can't do lunch today either. We're doing a project, and I just forgot something, so I need to grab it from upstairs." He motioned for Sage and Mel to go first.

"You... forgot something?" Cartier lowered the book. Mel felt her hands starting to stick with sweat as she realized forgetting something was probably a situation that never occurred for people their age. Lewis and Sage also stayed silent.

"Lewis," Cartier continued, "you can just say you're skipping school. You don't have to make up some half-baked excuse such as forgetting something. I also don't care, but you should follow the rules and go to school. But Mom leaves you be, so I won't say anything. As for lunch, though—Mom cares about getting together. You know this is routine. She may be okay with you skipping school sometimes, but she won't be happy with you skipping our weekly lunches." She then shrugged and closed her eyes, "But you can dig your own grave. Best get out of here before Mom comes back if you're going to skip." Cartier turned her attention back to the yellow book.

Lewis backed away from the kitchen toward the stairs when the front door lock clicked, and the door opened.

"Lunch is here!" Lewis's mom announced as she entered. "Oh!" She saw Mel and Sage standing a few steps up the stairs. "You brought guests, Lewis?"

"Oh, hi, Mom. Yes, this is Mel, my classmate, and her younger sister Sage."

"That's not his classmate, Mom," Cartier interrupted from her seat. Lewis whipped his head around to face her. Cartier happened to look up at that moment and saw him glaring. "What? That's not your classmate, Lewis. Am I not telling the truth? I know every face in our school system as class president, and of course, I'd recognize all the faces of my brother's classmates. I don't know why you'd lie. The first time you brought them around, I thought they were friends from another sector you some-how made."

"First time you brought them around?" Lewis's mom echoed. "When was that?" She was waiting for Lewis to answer.

Cartier seemed to realize she'd gotten Lewis in trou-ble, so she stayed silent. Sometimes, there is a sibling pact you don't break with the parents. Mel eyed Cartier sympathetically.

Lewis dipped his head. "Yesterday. I met them in another sector and brought them back, but you weren't home yet, Mom. Sorry for hiding the truth from you."

Lewis's mom pursed her lips before saying, "It's very unlike you to say an untruth, Lewis. I also don't condone you skipping school often. I wasn't aware you did that yesterday. But seeing as we have guests," she smiled graciously at Mel and Sage before turning back to him, "you and I will discuss this later. For now, let's have lunch, and your friends should join us. Will you, girls?"

Mel heard Sage take in a large gulp.

"Yes, of course, Mrs. Trisham. It's very kind of you to offer. We're sorry to intrude," Mel said, understanding there was no declining her offer.

"Not at all!" She beamed. "I do visitations to other sectors from time to time, but we don't often meet children on my visits, so it's exciting to hear what your sector is like if you don't mind indulging me over lunch." Lewis's mom hung up her keys and coat. "Lewis," she snapped, "help take this bag to the kitchen and set the table. I need to whip up some extra food now that we have guests."

Lewis obediently grabbed the large bag of takeout food that his mom brought and shuffled to the kitchen. Mel saw Cartier apologetically mouth a 'sorry' to Lewis while getting up to help him set the table, but before she could observe more, Mrs. Trisham had put a hand on her back through the railings of the stairs and gently pushed her and Sage back down.

"I'm Lewis's mom. You can call me 'Mrs. Trisham.' What are your names?"

"I'm Sage, and this is Mel," Sage introduced themselves. "We're, uh, from another sector." Mel wished they had more time to hash out a story together because they were both pulling from thin air.

"Excellent. Which sector, if you don't mind me asking? Your parents know you're both here, right?" Mrs. Trisham had brought them to the kitchen island and had them both sit on bar stools.

"Sector 10!" Lewis said over the sounds of him wrestling with the emptied paper bag to fold it. Mel was grateful that he responded.

"Oh, that's not too far," Mrs. Trisham said. "I've been there often enough that I know most families there. Which family are you from?"

"What do you mean?" Sage asked before Lewis could intervene again. Cartier shot them a funny look.

"Of course, I mean, what's your last name, silly," Mrs. Trisham chided. "You should know we recognize people by family names..."

Mel was breaking into a cold sweat now. *Do we make up a name? Use our own name? It'll be obvious we're not from there if she really knows all the families there.* She glanced at Lewis for help but saw he was avoiding eye contact. Mel shut her eyes tightly.

"Yu," she said quietly, but the sounds of Mrs. Trisham washing her hands drowned Mel out.

"Sorry, what was that?"

"Yu," Mel said more loudly. *Might as well just use our real name. I have no idea what name to even make up...*

"Yu?" Mrs. Trisham echoed while squinting. "I haven't heard of a family by that name."

Sage grabbed Mel's hand beneath the counter.

"But I probably simply forgot!" Mrs. Trisham said lightly. "Well, as I'm whipping up a chicken potato salad, tell me a bit more about yourselves. What's school like in your sector?"

"Mom!" Lewis said exasperatedly, "Can you stop bothering them with questions?" but he quieted when his mom shot him a look.

"Check your attitude, Lewis Trisham. You and I still need to talk later." With that tone change, Mel could see how Lewis's mom was a respected, top-marine biologist for the government.

"Sorry about that, ladies," Mrs. Trisham said to them. "What were you going to say before we were interrupted?"

Mel racked her brains on what she'd recently learned at school. "Um, I had a history class recently. We learned about premodern and prehistoric societies, like the Bronze Age around the twelfth century BCE. It was neat to read about world developments."

"Bronze Age?" Cartier questioned. "That's not a common curriculum for your age group. It's such an insignificant period compared to other periods we have in our history. Did you learn about this, Lewis?"

Mel's stomach dropped. She hadn't realized that in the Second Layer, their history could be different from the history she knew.

Lewis looked at them. "Um, no. Not yet! Maybe it's coming up soon for us."

Cartier slightly pouted. "I don't think so. I know every age group's curriculum since I'm class president, of course. I take this seriously because if I get noticed, it might set me up for a job at the GMA." Mel was getting annoyed at Cartier voicing everything but also impressed Cartier knew so much. *How much does she remember, and why does she keep exposing us!*

"I'm pretty sure Mom can get you a job at the GMA if you wanted." Lewis rolled his eyes. He playfully and loudly whispered to Sage, who was closer to him, "Cartier's *always* talking about working for the government. It's her *dream*." He said the last word goofily, resulting in Cartier smacking the back of his head.

"Ow!" Lewis rubbed his head.

"Mom's a scientist. I want to work in the offices where they make the rules. I want to work for Prime Minister Gio Bellows. That's different from what Mom does. Plus, I don't want to depend on Mom. I want to make it myself." Cartier looked off in the distance. Lewis was about to talk back, but Mrs. Trisham interrupted.

"All right, you two. Cut it out. Cartier, that's a great dream. I'm glad you're working on your own merit. Lewis, stop making fun of her. It's an honest dream. It's great that she wants to work for the Prime Minister, even if it's only because he's strikingly handsome." She grinned mischievously at the last bit.

"Mom!" Cartier stomped her foot. "Ugh, you two don't understand me!" She stormed upstairs to her room.

Lewis and his mom exchanged a look and broke out laughing. Mel didn't expect Mrs. Trisham to make a dig at Cartier, and she, too, found herself caught in the contagious laughter. Sage was also roaring with tears in her eyes.

When they all finished, Mrs. Trisham said to Lewis, "This doesn't mean you're off the hook. We're still talking later about you speaking an untruth. But I just couldn't help myself when Cartier said she wants to work for the

Prime Minister!" She put the large bowl of potato salad mixed with strips of rotisserie chicken on the island. "Help yourselves," she said to Mel and Sage. "Cartier is right, though. It's strange your school would teach the Bronze Age of all things. The timeframe also isn't right—it started much earlier than the twelfth century BCE."

"Mel wouldn't be wrong!" Sage said between mouthfuls. Mel hadn't noticed Sage already was gorging on the food. "She's top of her class," Sage continued. "Our mom says she's going to achieve great things!"

Mel felt her cheeks getting red with embarrassment at such a pure compliment.

"Maybe I just remembered wrong," she said sheepishly.

"Oh?" Mrs. Trisham raised a brow, and her eyes steeled. "You remembered... wrong?"

Lewis and Sage stopped eating, and when Mel realized what she'd done, it took everything in her to not gasp in horror. *I literally just told her I could remember things wrong. There's no way someone my age would remember something wrong in this layer!* Dread seeped into every bone of her body. *I just suggested the impossible to her. Is she going to realize we're not from here?*

CHAPTER 16

Mrs. Trisham eyed them warily after Mel's careless statement, the traces of hospitality and smile lines momentarily gone.

"Then perhaps... your teacher taught you the wrong dates," Mrs. Trisham slowly said while looking between Mel and Sage. "You're from the Yu family in Sector 10, was it? I'll inquire. I really can't imagine why they'd teach about the Bronze Age... unless you're not from around here," Mrs. Trisham mused. Mel, Sage, and Lewis didn't dare let out a breath. "But that's preposterous!" she laughed. "Anyway, I'd argue that the Coral Age is much more important to cover. I may bring this up to the Sector 10 school board. I have a few government contacts there."

Lewis suddenly got to his feet and put his dishes away. "Ah, yes, you best do that, Mom. I'll remind you if you forget. Thank you for lunch! We actually need to rush back to school—our own respective schools, that is. I just need to get something from upstairs." He hastily grabbed Sage's and Mel's bowls and put them away. "I'll wash the dishes later, Mom!" He gestured for Mel and Sage to follow him.

Mel immediately got up. She was pretty sure her socks were soaked from nervous sweat. "Yes, thank you, Mrs. Trisham, for the hospitality. Lunch was delicious!"

"Thank you, ma'am!" Sage followed suit. All three of them dashed upstairs before Mrs. Trisham could say much else. When Mel finally caught her breath and calmed her nerves (mostly from the heart palpitations she was having from Mrs. Trisham's conversation), she saw the messy desk and shelves filled with books and knickknacks. Lewis had brought them to his dad's office and shut the door.

"We've lost enough time. Once I grab the box we're here for, let's head back out." Lewis confidently walked to the corner of the room and started digging through a chest of trinkets and parts.

A knock sounded at the door, followed by Cartier's voice. "Lewis, why are you in Dad's office? I thought you said you were grabbing something for school. You know we're not allowed to take Dad's stuff out."

"Yeah, I know. Mind your own business!" Lewis grunted as he pulled items out of the chest.

Cartier opened the door a sliver. "What are you doing? Actually, never mind. Go ahead and impress your girlfriends with Dad's stuff. But seriously, if you don't want to get into further trouble with Mom, don't take stuff out of the house."

"What?" Mel and Sage said simultaneously. *Girlfriends?* Mel felt her cheeks warming, but Lewis seemed unfazed.

"So, what if I am? At least I have someone."

The next thing Mel knew, Cartier had run back to her room sobbing.

"Wait, no, Cartier! I didn't mean that!" Lewis stopped rummaging in the box and called after her. "I'm sorry! It's okay not to have a partner! You got a whole life ahead of you! You got to be happy on your own first! Ugh!" He ran his hands through his dark hair.

"That was mean of you," Sage openly pointed out, crossing her arms.

"I know!" Lewis responded. "I'm just operating on auto-pilot right now and trying to get that box." He turned back toward the chest. "I'll talk to Cartier later."

Mel flipped through some open notebooks on his dad's desk as he rummaged. Most of the book was filled with gibberish sketches, numbers, and lines until she flipped to a largely empty page with one written sentence, passion-ately circled in the center: *How to get to the other layers?*

Just then, the doorbell downstairs rang. "Coming," Mrs. Trisham sang. They heard her open the door.

"Oh, you're not Enforcer Jovanna. How may I help you, Enforcer?"

Sage turned to Lewis. "I thought you said Enforcer Jovanna is your sector's enforcer, right? The one we met at the park?"

"Yeah, it should be him." Lewis furrowed his brows. "There's no reason why it would be another enforcer. Even if he's sick, it would be someone else that my mom would recognize." The man at the door was speaking, so they padded softly to the doorway of the office to eavesdrop.

"Yes. We see this house is registered to a Trisham fam-ily. You must be Mrs. Trisham?"

"Dr. Leo-Trisham," Lewis's mom corrected the enforcer. "I'm a marine biologist for the GMA. What may I help you with?"

"Apologies, ma'am." Mel didn't think he sounded sorry. "Do you mind if we come inside?"

"I do mind, as a matter of fact." Her voice was steely compared to her previously bright countenance. "You need to inform me of the intent of your visit. From the embroidery on your uniform, I see you're the prime minister's special enforcers. How can I help you?"

"Mel!" Sage whispered. "They caught up!"

Mel's stomach felt queasy. "Lewis, have you found the box yet?"

"Not yet, but it's definitely in this pile of junk." Lewis ran back to the corner to search.

Downstairs, Mel could hear more.

"I expected a GMA scientist such as yourself to know of us. We received reports of suspicious activity in the area. Have you noticed anything strange?"

"Suspicious? I haven't noticed anything."

"Nothing out of the ordinary?"

"Can you inform me what this is about?" Dr. Leo-Trisham demanded firmly but calmly downstairs.

The enforcer at the doorway cleared his throat. "Well, seeing as you also work for the GMA, Dr. Leo-Trisham, I can say we've received system alerts of... others... in this neighborhood."

"Others?" She sounded exasperated.

"Yes. People who don't belong. That's the extent I can share. Unfortunately, anything else is classified."

Mel noticed Cartier's head sticking out of her bedroom door, listening intently to the downstairs conversation. Cartier turned her head and saw Mel, and a look of fear formed on her face. She quickly collected herself again and walked out toward Mel. Cartier came to the office, ignored Mel, and addressed Lewis. "Can you come out here for a moment? I need to speak with you."

"Found it!" Lewis held the same exact box they saw in Romilda's memory victoriously over his head.

"Lewis, a word?" Cartier repeated.

Lewis still felt bad about his insensitive remark to his sister earlier and agreed. He handed the box to Sage on his way out. "I'll be right back. I just need to apologize to her."

Cartier shut the door once Lewis entered the hallway with her, but it wasn't difficult to listen to their hushed whispers when Mel pressed her ear against the shut door. She motioned for Sage to join her.

"Lewis, did you *hear* why those enforcers are here? Who they're looking for?"

"No, I was a bit busy." He played dumb. "Who are they looking for?"

"They're not just any enforcers, Lewis. They're the prime minister's special task force! Mom noted their uniform! Prime Minister Gio's people." She sounded breathy and excited.

"Okay, and?"

"Lewis, don't pretend you don't know. They said they're looking for people that don't belong. This is a special ask from the prime minister, and those two friends of yours are highly suspicious."

"What are you saying, Cartier? That I don't even know who my friends are? They're just from another sector," Lewis whispered defensively.

"No, I don't think so. You met them while skipping school. They're not in our school system. They keep acting surprised we remember things that are so easy to remember with our memories. Mel literally just said she probably remembered *wrongly* about what she learned at school. That never happens. No one even fathoms it because it just doesn't. You know this, Lewis."

"Okay, yes, that's true," Lewis acquiesced. "It is indeed very strange. I'm sure it was just a joke, or she felt embarrassed her curriculum was different."

There was a pause during which Mel could imagine Cartier glaring Lewis down. Cartier finally spoke again. "I think you know it, too, Lewis. Either you're turning a blind eye, and I don't know why. Or you already know and for some reason don't want to admit it. But have it your way. They're your friends. But be careful, Lewis. We don't know who or what they are if they're not from here." Cartier sounded deflated as her footsteps receded back to her room.

Lewis opened the office door only to have Mel and Sage fall at his feet. He looked down at them. "You heard everything?"

Mel and Sage nodded.

"You trust us... right?" Sage asked.

"What do you mean?"

"Everything Cartier said about not knowing who we are and to be careful. You trust us, right?"

Lewis took a long look at them before answering, "I do. We've been in this from the very beginning. I'm sure you would feel the same about me if our roles were switched. If I were the one who stumbled into your world, the First Layer."

Mel felt herself well up, but before she could respond, Sage burst forward and hugged Lewis. He had a look of surprise but then broke into a laugh before he became serious again.

"We have to go ASAP. If Cartier pieced together that those special enforcers are looking for you two, my mom most definitely knows."

"But I think your mom is turning them away." Sage pulled herself out of the hug and helped Mel up. Sure enough, Mel heard Mrs. Trisham bidding the enforcer goodbye and shutting the door.

"Sage is right. They're leaving!" Mel agreed.

Suddenly, Mrs. Trisham called out from below. "Lewis! Mel, Sage! If you got what you needed for school, come by the kitchen first before you leave!"

All three of them exchanged looks.

"Don't worry," Lewis finally said. "It's my mom." He headed out of the office and down the hall. As he passed his room, he popped inside to grab a backpack.

"I think she knows." Mel turned to Sage.

"What should we do? She's probably telling us to stop by the kitchen to prevent us from leaving, and then she'll hold us up!" Sage whispered back.

"Hurry up. We have to go," Lewis called from the stairwell as he hastily stuffed the box into the backpack. They made to follow, but Mel whispered back to Sage in private.

"I'm not sure why she didn't tell the enforcers at the door, but she probably wants to get to the bottom of it. We just need to stick together."

"What about Lewis?"

Mel thought for a moment. "No matter what, she's his mom. He's going to trust her, and she'll protect him. She won't do that for us, though. He might change his mind about us if she convinces him. Or even if he doesn't change his mind, it'll put him in a difficult position. We have to be prepared to leave without him if it comes to it."

"Leave him behind?" Shock laced Sage's voice. "He's helped us so much, though."

"Yeah, but he's from this layer, Sage. We're not. At the end of the day, the Prime Minister just wants us." Mel felt the horror creep into her stomach as she recognized the truth to her own statement. *What will they do with us? Separate us? Keep us locked up? Run experiments on us?* Mel shook her head to dispel those thoughts. She had to keep it together for Sage. She turned to face her sister, stopped them on the stairs, and put both hands on her shoulders. "As long as we are together, Sage. It's you and me."

Sage looked Mel in the eyes and nodded. She knew no matter who they left behind, they had to stick together.

Mel took a deep breath. "Let's see what Mrs. Trisham wants. Lewis still has the box on him, too."

They arrived downstairs to see Mrs. Trisham and Lewis waiting for them.

"You wanted to see us, Mrs. Trisham?" Mel asked as they approached the kitchen.

"I was just asking Lewis if there's anything he wants to tell me. And now I'd like to ask you two whether there's something you'd like to share?"

Mel looked to Lewis for any indication of what he said. *Did he tell his mom the truth? Or did he make something up? I need to make sure my story matches up.* He only looked at her with pursed lips and shifty eyes.

"I told Lewis to not speak until after you've answered, so you don't need to look at him. I just had special task force enforcers at my house, and I'd like to ask if you two have anything to do with it," Dr. Leo-Trisham sternly added.

Mel reached out to hold Sage's hand. She was ready to bolt with her. *Forget about Grandpa's box and key. I'd rather get away, find Romilda again, and demand she tell us how to use the vending machine to get home.* Mel remained silent, and for once, Sage did as well.

After what felt like forever, Mrs. Trisham heaved a big sigh. "Look. Lewis said just as much as you two—nothing. So, you're going to show me what you have in that backpack." She shifted her gaze to Lewis.

"Mom!" he protested.

"You're all hiding something, and whatever's in there is part of it. You're not leaving the house until you show me." She crossed her arms resolutely.

Lewis gingerly placed his backpack onto the kitchen island, and they all gathered around it. He reached inside and pulled out the locked, metal box.

"Well... show me what's inside. That key off Mel's neck would fit, no?"

Mel hadn't wanted to let her know she had the key, but Dr. Leo-Trisham's keen eyes did not miss the dangling token on her neck. Mel took off the necklace as Lewis turned the box around to face her.

She brought it to the box's lock and held her breath, hovering the key right outside the keyhole. *This is it—everything that's happened so far. The answers are in here.* She inserted it and twisted it in one motion. They heard a satisfying click inside and opened it. A box that had remained sealed for forty years, protecting its secret.

Mel's heart sank.

"A piece of paper?" Sage exhaled in disbelief. "Where's the device?" Mel shushed her as Dr. Leo-Trisham was still present, but the doctor had picked up something else within the box.

"Device? You mean this tape recorder?" she questioned.

Lewis caught Mel's gaze with a look of confusion reflecting her own. *Did Romilda mention a tape recorder? Where's Grandpa's device?*

Dr. Leo-Trisham pressed the 'play' button on the recorder to be met with a familiar voice.

"To whoever managed to open this," it started.

"Hold on, Mom, isn't this your voice?" Lewis interrupted, but his mom's expression froze in silent alarm, and the recording continued.

"My name is Dr. Leo-Trisham, and my husband, Dr. Carlisle Trisham, replicated the key to this box after years of studying it. If you opened it and hear this message, I'll assume you have the original key: Howler's key. I must report regretfully that the original content of this box was seized by none other than the Prime Minister. Special enforcers searched my husband's office very soon after we opened the box. They claimed they didn't take anything, but the item was gone after they left. Why would they pretend? Because they don't want to admit that it exists or that it is important to them..."

The three of them looked at each other and at Mrs. Trisham's immobile frame.

"My husband subsequently disappeared. So, I must record this message before I forget and lose it... for him and for our future. The item within this box was Howler's device to refine the power stones that run our vending portals. The GMA has kept his technology under wraps, and it's quite complex. But Howler was able to simplify the process by inventing this portable device that could produce a power stone within mere hours. This changes *everything*. It would enable easier access to portals and to the First Layer as well as shift the monopoly that the GMA has on this tech." The voice paused and got quieter. "But we failed. We failed in keeping this safe, and now my husband is missing. I ask of you, please, to acquire it back. I'm too close to the GMA and am now under supervision, so my hands are tied. Please do what I can't and bring the device back to where it belongs, with the Mastodons. May the waters guide you."

The four of them stood listening to the static at the end of the message, flabbergasted.

"Mom," Lewis broke the silence tentatively, "are you a Mastodon? What happened to Dad?"

"The Prime Minister stole Grandpa's device?" Sage said hopelessly.

"I... don't know," Mrs. Trisham responded, her shaky voice revealing the conflict brewing within her. "This message must be from years ago when your dad disappeared. I don't remember this... How can I not remember this?"

"Why're you crying, Mom?" Lewis hastily grabbed some tissues and handed them to her. She touched her wet face in bewilderment.

What's going on! Thoughts chaotically flew through Mel's mind, but at that moment, a deep voice sounded from outside through loudspeakers.

"We know you're in there." All four of them jumped. "We demand you come out and turn yourselves in, unverified Envoys. Dr. Leo-Trisham, if you do not turn them in, we'll charge you as complicit in harboring persons of interest and posing a threat to national security." It was the special enforcer who was at the door! He didn't leave for some reason and was now demanding they turn themselves in!

There was a moment of silence as the situation sunk in.

Then Mrs. Trisham sprang into action. She turned and stooped down to a kitchen cabinet next to the sink, opened it, and started throwing out the various bottles of household cleaners that were previously sitting inside. "Lewis, take the girls out of here. They're looking for them."

Wait. She's not turning us in?

"Mom, what're you doing? We have nowhere to go! Also, just... what!"

The enforcer outside announced again, "We have your house surrounded. There's nowhere else to go. Come out now, and we'll keep it cordial."

Lewis's mom turned to them with fierce determination in her eyes. "There's a secret passageway from under this sink. Go down and follow the path. It'll take you out of an opening a few houses down. It doesn't get you far, but it'll get you out of here. Just be careful they don't see you when you're exiting the tunnel." She lifted the bottom panel of the emptied cabinet and revealed an abyss.

"Since when did we have this secret tunnel? What's going on? Why aren't you asking us more questions?" Mel had never heard Lewis so rattled.

"Lewis, these aren't normal enforcers. They're the Prime Minister's enforcers. They don't show often, and when they do, it means trouble. Any memory that people have of them is either forgotten or those people are never seen again. They will *not* be lenient. You all need to leave. I will go out to buy you some time."

"Wait, Mom, how do you know about these special enforcers and what they do if people forget them? And what about you?" Lewis's voice was raising in pitch as uncertainty steeped into it. Mrs. Trisham had already walked to Mel and Sage and pulled them to the cabinet.

Sage was the first to go into the tunnel. She looked back at Mel and understood the look Mel was giving. *It's an exit. We'll take it.* She sat at the edge and stuck her legs down, carefully lowering herself into the abyss. Mel was next.

"Mom!" Lewis prompted Mrs. Trisham. She turned to him and kneeled to his eye level.

"Lewis. You need to stay calm. Take a deep breath." He did as he was told.

"Good. Now, listen carefully. Your father was working on great things, and a part of it was allowing travel between our world and another. Something I think you're already aware of." She glanced at Mel.

Mel quickly looked away. She felt like they were sharing a private moment, and she shouldn't listen in, but she was still waiting for Sage to get to the bottom of the tunnel.

"The recording triggered some of my memory recall, but we don't have much time for me to explain in depth. After your father disappeared, I kept this from you, Cartier, the world, and even from myself. But know this. Our government is indeed flawed, but it's also doing its best. No place is perfect. Your father dedicated his life to making our society better in his own way. I chose a different route and dedicated my life to the government to help, but in this case, the Prime Minister is now coming for you, my family. Just because he has Mel and Sage doesn't mean he won't come for you because you have had close contact with them. You'll be closely monitored for the rest of your life, like invisible shackles for as long as you'll remember. In this, I cannot trust these enforcers. You need to run with Mel and Sage. Get to the contact who's been helping you. I trust your father."

At this point, Sage was already at the bottom, and Mel was partially lowered into the tunnel. Mrs. Trisham pushed Lewis toward the cabinet. "Go now. I'll put the paneling and items back into the cabinet. Then I'll go distract them."

Mel reached the bottom of the tunnel. There were horizontal bars along a wall after they lowered themselves to help them climb down. The tunnel was dark, but there were small lights along the bottom of the path, illuminating the way like the aisles of an airplane. She looked up to see Lewis's legs coming down as well.

"Mom, you knew about Dad? That he was part of the Mastodons? You know about the government using memories?"

"Shhh, Lewis! You can't say things like that out loud. Just leave. And know, I love you. So much. Now go!" Mrs. Trisham shut the cabinet floor back into place in Lewis's face.

"Mom!" Lewis pounded on the flooring that was above him. "Mom!" But she didn't open it.

PART THREE

CHAPTER 17

After much coaxing to get Lewis to come down, he mutely followed Mel and Sage down the winding dirt passageway toward the exit.

The exit was at the foot of a large juniper tree a few houses down, covered by a ring of bushes planted around the tree. Mel peeked out first and saw from afar the official cars surrounding that cute, pale blue house of Lewis's. Mrs. Trisham had walked out with both hands up and was approaching the enforcers.

"Aren't they holding the same kind of ropes that Romilda had?" Lewis crouched next to her.

Mel looked more closely, and sure enough, the enforcers had the same glowing, snakelike ropes in their hands. "You've never seen those before, Lewis?"

He shook his head. "No. Community enforcers aren't armed at all. Seeing it on Romilda was the first time I've encountered it."

"Are they magical?" Sage piped up as she scooted next to Mel to see as well.

"I doubt it," Lewis responded. "To you, our memory serums and rooms probably seem a bit magical, right? Given that Romilda had placed her ropes in a tank on her submarine, I'd imagine the ropes are somehow derived from or enhanced by some sort of marine life, but I had no idea we even had this technology."

Mel was in awe. The Second Layer was full of technological advancements that stemmed from their marine research.

"Hold on, is that... your sister, Lewis?" Sage suddenly asked.

"No way, they got Cartier too?" Lewis said with concern.

"No... it looks like she's talking to them. Over there, next to that car. Probably with the lead enforcer?" Sage pointed out.

Mel looked to where Sage described and saw a scene that made her stomach drop. Cartier was comfortably chatting with the enforcer who had the loudspeaker. The other enforcers had swarmed Lewis's mom, sending their snakelike ropes out to bind her hands in front of her. The lead enforcer then approached her to talk. Mrs. Trisham responded by shaking her head. Mel imagined she was probably telling them she had no idea what they were talking about because after that, the lead enforcer looked back at Cartier, who got really worked up, waving her hands frantically as if trying to persuade them. Mrs. Trisham's face betrayed no shock, but when Mel turned to Lewis, his face was frozen in a mixture of anger, surprise, and hurt.

"There's no way Cartier told them about us, Lewis." Mel tried to appease him. She was also shocked, but it was easier for her to digest as she wasn't very fond of Cartier.

"It looks quite clear from here." Lewis's face darkened. "She sold us out. She sold Mom out!" He turned to Mel and Sage. "You know why? Because she wants that government job as the Prime Minister's personal monkey! She sold us out so she could get what she wants." He was crawling out from under the cover of the bushes, "Well, you know what? She won't get it. I'm going to save Mom!"

Mel lunged and grabbed him by the waist to hold him back. "And do what? She's surrounded by enforcers! The best way we can help is to get to Romilda." Lewis struggled against her. "Romilda should help us get your mom back in exchange for the box and key! She's skilled enough to take them," Mel added as she thought about their first encounter with Romilda.

Lewis pushed Mel off forcefully but had stopped trying to run. "You're right. If I went, it'd be in vain." His fists remained clenched, though. "Let's get the box to Romilda."

But right at that moment, to Mel's sinking horror, Cartier happened to look their way and saw Lewis and Mel sprawled on the ground. There was a glint of hesitation in her eyes before she pointed them out to the lead enforcer, yelling, "They're over there! They have my brother!"

"Run!" Mel yelled. They scrambled to their feet, with Sage getting her sleeves tangled in the bush branches, momentarily slowing them down. They sprinted toward the stairwell down the cliffs.

Romilda, you said you'd be watching. Where are you? The enforcers were gaining on them. Mel could hear the whipping of the glowing ropes striking the air close behind them as the enforcers threw them. They were nearing the stairwell when Mel suddenly heard some forceful grunts and the sound of slamming bodies behind her. She glanced behind to behold a bizarre sight.

The enforcers piled, one behind the other like a sandwich, with the lead enforcer at the forefront, his face smushed in midair. It was as if they'd run into an invisible wall! A figure then appeared before Mel, Sage, and Lewis and quickly stepped around the three of them to face the enforcers.

"Hurry down the stairs to the shoreline." It was distorted but undeniably Romilda's voice, and she had her hood back on. Mel's heart leaped with hope. *She's here!* A hooded Romilda tossed them two walkie-talkies. "The wall I put up only holds for a specified area, so this won't stop the enforcers from going around it once they get back to their senses. You have the token and box now—keep them both safe! Get moving!" Romilda urged as she reached into her trench coat and took out her own set of glowing, writhing ropes. "I've sent a mayday ping on our systems to any Mastodon who's still listening. There's no telling who'll respond, but worth a shot. I have faith someone will come forth to help. You need to run now!"

"No way, a member of the Mastodons? I thought they all disappeared." The lead enforcer cracked his neck as he got up. His angry eyes locked with Mel's. "Get them!" He roared at the others while they scrambled up.

"You'll have to get through me first." Out of the corner of her eyes, as she ran, Mel saw Romilda shoot the rope out as if it had a life of its own and tie itself around the feet of two enforcers, tripping them.

The three of them got to the beach. No one had followed them, so Mel assumed Romilda was successfully holding them off. *But for how long?*

"Where are we supposed to go?" Sage asked. "Do we wait for Romilda at her submarine?"

Lewis put a hand above his eyes, searching the waters. "I don't see it. Do you?"

Mel and Sage also shook their heads. Looking across the water, there was no sign of the submarine nor a hint of where it'd be. It was no surprise the submarine was well-hidden, but Mel wished Romilda had given them a hint before she faced the enforcers.

They suddenly heard a commotion from the cliffs above. "Get them!" It was the lead enforcer's voice.

What happened to Romilda?

Sage also heard and looked back at Mel and Lewis in fear. "They're coming!" She made to run for the water. "We have to find her submarine to hide!"

"Hold on, Sage!" Lewis reached out and wrapped his arms around her. "If we run out there now, there's no guarantee we can find the submarine, *and* the enforcers would clearly see us. We're now standing against the cliffs, so looking out, they can't see us yet. We need to stay along the cliffs."

"And what? They're coming down. We need to at least try instead of just stand here and do nothing!" She grabbed Sage's hand and gave a squeeze. For once, she agreed with Sage.

"There's a hidden cave," Lewis said matter-of-factly. "I used to play here all the time. This way." He started walking away from the stairs. Mel forgot this area must have been like a backyard for Lewis, what with his house right there.

"Remember to stick to the walls, quickly!" Lewis prompted them urgently as the yelling and sounds of steps above got nearer. They followed Lewis until he disappeared when rounding the corner of a jutting rock.

"Where did he—" A hand shot out from within the rock and yanked them inside.

Light streamed in from the crack. Mel looked back outside and saw that Lewis had pulled them through a crack between rocks. The crack was just big enough for them, but no adult would be able to fit through.

"Where are we?" Sage whispered.

"It's my secret hideaway," Lewis responded with a smile. "Gosh, I haven't been here in so long. It's the exact same. Let's get farther inside so we can talk more openly without them hearing us."

The enforcers were causing a ruckus on the beach, yelling at each other to spread out. They'd made it inside the cave just in time. Mel found that the cave was just big enough for the three of them to stand upright, but it was quite narrow.

In a single file, they followed Lewis toward the back before she felt the space open into a larger pocket, but it was pitch black now that they were deeper within. There was some rustling and clicking but then light flooded the pocket they were in. Lewis was stooped next to a small electric lamp.

"Glad I left this here long ago!" He'd plopped himself onto the sandy ground and took off his backpack. Mel and Sage sat as well. From here, they could no longer hear the enforcers outside. In the low light, Mel could make out some drawings on the walls. Drawings of a little boy with a man.

"Did you draw these, Lewis?"

He looked around as well. "I did back then. I don't have many memories of my dad, and we don't have many, if any, photos together. So, I made my own memories here." He looked down into his lap. "Kind of pitiful, right?"

Mel scooted forward and, without thinking, reached for his hand resting in his lap and held it. She wanted to say it was not pitiful but also didn't know what to say, so she just held it and looked at his face earnestly in the dimly lit room, hoping her feelings came across. He looked up at her and smiled thankfully. Mel found herself blushing and immediately pulled back her hand.

"So, what're we going to do?" Sage prodded Lewis's backpack.

That's right! The whole point of them going back, Lewis's mom protecting them, and Romilda fighting for them, was to get Grandpa's box! But the whole plan is ruined because the Prime Minister has the device...

Lewis pulled the backpack to his lap and took out the box and its contents.

"Wow." Mel touched the box. "This belonged to Grandpa." She imagined Grandpa holding it decades ago. Her other hand unconsciously reached for the key around her neck. Lewis was staring intensely at the tape recorder with his mom's message. Because the two of them were engrossed in these items, they forgot about the seemingly inconsequential piece of paper also inside the box.

"Hey, I think there's something on this paper," Sage announced as she picked it up. Mel and Lewis snapped back from their internal thoughts and gathered around her. "It's a drawing of a machine?" It looked like a tiny submarine on four legs with a pipe out the side that led to a tray with a transparent dome.

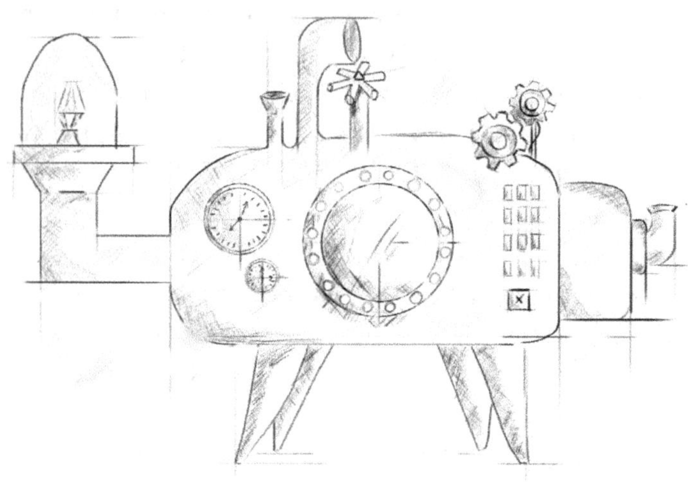

Dr. Carlisle Trisham's sketch of Howler's device.

Lewis's eyes widened, and he snatched the paper out of her hands to get a closer look. "I've seen this before!"

"So what?" Mel felt an indescribable emotion bubbling inside her. *No more! I'm tired of this. There's always more and more. Things aren't going to plan! Romilda's whereabouts are unknown, the device is with the Prime Minister, Lewis's mom is captured, and I have no idea how to get Sage and myself home. There's always been an answer, a way out, or a next step.* But here, she couldn't think of what to do next.

"There's nothing to do now." She struggled to hold back angry tears as all hope felt lost.

"This is a sketch of your grandpa's device, and I know where it is." Lewis examined the drawing.

"What do you mean?" Mel snapped. "We all know it's in the Prime Minister's hands. Your dad and mom didn't know or tell us where exactly it is, and now she's asking us to get it back? How can we do something they couldn't?"

"Because I have a photographic memory," Lewis retorted. "There's a magazine issue from last week, and it had a shot of the Prime Minister in his office. He's known for rotating the items in his office, but his collection is so vast I haven't seen a repeated item ever."

"Do you mean...?" Sage slapped two hands to her face.

"Yeah," he said simply. "It's on his shelf."

Mel gawked at Lewis in a stupor. "Are you sure?"

He gave her an impatient look. "One hundred percent clarity. Remember?" He rapped his head lightly. "This sketch is unmistakably the item I saw in the magazine photo, which means it must be the device."

Sage turned her head to Mel with wide eyes. "We can go save Grandpa's device."

"Grandpa's device doesn't need saving. *We* need saving!" Mel gestured wildly at themselves.

When Mel looked back at Sage, she was surprised to see Sage's eyes burning with fierce conviction. "This is for Grandpa. And we need it to get back home. His device can charge those vending portals." Mel had never seen Sage so serious, and it threw her off guard.

"I don't know." Mel hesitated. *If it's in the Prime Minister's office, are they saying we need to break into it? We're going to get caught!*

"We can fulfill my parents' wish for us to retrieve it!" Lewis agreed with Sage.

"Look," Mel faced them, "are you two thinking this through? Do you even know what you're saying we'll do? This is dangerous!"

"Come on, Mel. We have to get it. We know where it is, and it's exactly where they're keeping my mo—" Lewis objected.

"No, we don't! We need to sit back. We don't have to infiltrate his office. This is more than what we signed up for. We were just supposed to get Romilda this box. We did it. That's it." Mel was scared. Up to this point, they'd kept a distance from enforcers and from the GMA, but now, they'd be walking straight into the lion's den.

"We'd think of a plan," Lewis added. "We'll be ready."

"Why? Why do we need to go?" Mel was getting worked up, and Lewis fell silent and looked away.

Sage shuffled over to sit next to Mel and put a hand on her knee. "We have to go to help Mrs. Trisham. To help Romilda. They were all taken by those enforcers while they were protecting us. We have a chance now to help them. Lewis was saying earlier that the Prime Minister's office would also be the same place they're keeping his mom. Probably Romilda too."

At that, Mel took a softer tone. "I'm scared, Sage. They'll take us just like Romilda and Mrs. Trisham." She looked into the eyes of her younger sister and saw a resolve mixed with lifted brows of worry.

"I'm scared too, Mel. But they need our help now. We're the only ones who know what happened to them. And we're the only ones with this recorded evidence. Lewis," she looked at Lewis, "needs our help getting his mom back." Mel looked at him too and saw how silently distraught he was. Sage continued, "He's been helping us in trying to get us home ever since we arrived. It's time we help him get *his* home back."

Mel took a shaky breath. *At the end of the day, we can't just leave Lewis alone. He was a friend who'd been with them through all of this. And Sage has a point about the recorded evidence as well. We're the only ones who know...*"Okay, let's do it. But we need plans and backup plans."

Sage beamed, and Lewis looked up in surprise.

"We'll have a plan. I won't say it won't be difficult and dangerous, but it'll be possible. I also recognize you don't have to do this. You could just leave me behind and try to get home, so I appreciate what you're doing here."

"Well, we can't really just go home..." Mel said in response. "Not with those special enforcers looking for us. It's probably best we try to save Mrs. Trisham and Romilda first to help us get home anyway." She grinned at Lewis. "Plus, you'd do the same for us."

Lewis's serious expression split into a wide smile at Mel's usage of his own words earlier.

The three of them brought their heads together and started plotting.

CHAPTER 18

Lewis peeked out of the cave's opening before turning back and giving Mel and Sage the signal to follow. According to Lewis, the Prime Minister's office is in the very same building in which his mom works, so Lewis was familiar with it. He'd also been inside the office on field trips, and fortunately, his class was having an excursion this afternoon there again. The plan was to join his class and in the middle of it, sneak off or stay behind in the Prime Minister's office, create a commotion so the security guards would leave their posts, and then grab the device off the shelf. They'd stuff it in their backpack and leave the building with the field trip group again. It sounded safe enough and doable to Mel.

Lewis had stepped out earlier to procure some uniforms for Mel and Sage. The first idea was to go back to his house and look for some of his sister's older uniforms that were too small now, but they realized Cartier may still be home, and the enforcers may be surveilling it. That's when Lewis suggested he go to his school's Unwanted Items corner. "It's stuff people pretend they forgot at school because they just don't want it. Usually homework, or an ugly lunch kit or something," Lewis had explained. *It's like a lost and found! Except… they don't actually lose things because of their incredible memories.*

In the past, he'd seen *lost* blazers there. Sometimes pants and tops if people didn't change back after gym and left their uniforms. "Kids often do it, so they don't have to wear a starchy, restrictive uniform for a few days before their parents procure another set. It's quite wasteful, but the school will recycle uniform materials if they find them lying around," Lewis had expounded before he left.

He had come back with two school blazers and one skort. "It's not everything, but if no one's looking carefully, you should fit in," he'd said as he handed the disguises to them. One of the blazers fit Mel quite nicely, but both were too large for Sage. The skort didn't fit either of them, so they left it behind.

Lewis led them to another stairwell up the cliffs. They agreed to take another one as the special enforcers may be watching the one they'd taken earlier. He checked his watch. "If we take the public bus to MAGMA headquarters, we should get there just in time while everyone's gathered at the front. After they count off and confirm they have every student, they'll usually steer everyone in. We can then insert ourselves. I'll see a few of my classmates, but no one really questions anything. They know I'm always up to things, so they don't think twice about stuff anymore."

Mel thought that was quite convenient for him. *Kind of unfair his propensity for skipping school and doing his own things rewards him in that people just let him do whatever he wants…*

They climbed the other stairwell and hit the main road. Mel glanced around nervously.

"I don't think they'd expect us to be taking a bus, so we should be fine. Nor will they expect us to be getting closer to the Prime Minister instead," Lewis said as he led them to a bus stop. It was the same bus stop that he took them to when they first met him. Mel looked at that vending machine, wondering how they got it to work that time. *It looks quite normal to me...*

Lewis noticed her looking and said, "You two really scared me when you used it. Did you even know what you were doing?"

"Not a clue," Sage responded, shaking her head. "We keep doing it by accident."

The bus arrived, and Lewis motioned for them to follow him. Once they boarded, to Mel's surprise, there was no steering wheel at the front. It just had one panel with some buttons. She brought her head to Lewis's ear as they sat.

"Where's the bus driver?"

He looked around to make sure no one was listening. The other riders were engrossed in their phones or books. In fact, many were reading that yellow booklet with Prime Minister Gio's beaming face on it. Mel shuddered.

Lewis put his arms around Mel and Sage, sitting on either side of him, bringing them closer to speak.

"I'm guessing the First Layer still has bus drivers? We don't. Been gone for a while. All of our public transit is automated."

"And there have never been any accidents?" Sage whispered.

"Nope. It's very safe. No pedestrian incidents or accidents with other automobiles. These are all set routes, and then it has sensors for anything that gets close. It also has weight and motion sensors at the entrance to gauge how many people are on board to ensure everyone gets off at the end of the day. Oh, and it's also free. Courtesy of the GMA."

The bus was now moving. Mel was relieved to get this moment to relax a little. *It feels like we've been running all day!* She fidgeted with Grandpa's key around her neck. Something pressed against her thigh, and when she looked down, she remembered she'd stuffed one of the walkie-talkies Romilda tossed them into her pocket. Sage had the other one since she tended to wander away. Lewis had the backpack ready to grab the device.

"What will we do when we get the device and get out?" Mel asked out loud.

Lewis shrugged. "Let's hope someone received that message for help that Romilda sent. Or there are notes on where they are keeping my mom and Romilda."

Mel nodded but anxiously mused, *So much can go wrong.* She fell into a fitful sleep, with thoughts running amok of everything that could go awry.

She woke to someone shaking her gently. "We're here." To her horror, she found her head resting on Lewis's shoulder, and... there was a wet spot where her head was! She groaned inwardly. *I drooled on him!*

"Thanks, Lewis." She got up hastily, hoping he wouldn't notice the wet spot. Sage had also fallen asleep with her head leaning against his other arm and groggily opened her eyes. Mel was glad she wasn't the only one. The three disembarked the bus to see a shiny, multiple-storied, glass building in front of them.

"Welcome to the MAGMA headquarters," Lewis said sarcastically.

The bottom section of the building was all white with massive glass doors at the entrance, but the top floors of the building looked to be completely transparent glass. They could see people in suits walking throughout, like a see-through microorganism.

"Is that your class, Lewis?" Sage pointed at a huddled group of children in navy blue blazers with a few adults herding.

"Yup. I think they're counting people, so we'll wait. Once they start moving toward the building, we can flow in with them. But before we go in," Lewis fished out the tape recorder and handed it to Sage, "you take this for safekeeping. You're less likely to be noticed by enforcers since you're not doing the actual device stealing like we are." She nodded and took it.

It wasn't long before the group started to move toward the doors, so the trio caught up and tailed at the end.

"Lewis?" One of the students happened to look behind and saw them. "I wasn't expecting to see you today. You usually skip field trips. Especially when it's government or aquarium-related." This classmate was slightly taller than Lewis and Mel, with a darker complexion and curly, brown hair.

"Hey, Marcus. I, too, am surprised I'm here. There's a first for everything," Lewis greeted him. "Meet Mel and Sage."

"You all talk funny," Sage blurted before she caught herself. Mel rolled her eyes and hoped Marcus wouldn't think much of the comment.

He shifted his gaze to Mel and Sage. Mel didn't like attention being brought to her and looked away, but Lewis had put a hand behind her back to push her forward with the group. She didn't realize she'd stopped walking. Marcus's gaze lingered on their slightly lacking uniforms before saying, "Nice to meet you two. I'm guessing Lewis extended an invite to you?"

"Yes, I invited them. Thought it'd be more fun."

Marcus's flawlessly pleasant face tightened into a frown that felt uncannily like that of an adult's disapproving gaze. "You should notify the adult chaperones, but..." Marcus broke into a dazzling smile, "it is more fun this way." He took Sage's hand. "Come along. You stick out like a sore thumb because you're not even our height. We just have to cover you from the chaperones." As Sage was led further into the group, Mel caught a glimpse of her wide eyes and beet-red cheeks at being taken by the hand of Lewis's charismatic friend.

Lewis grinned. "Thanks, Marcus." It seemed like his friends were cool with his shenanigans. The group entered the building, and Mel was in awe at how clean and high-tech it was. Back in her town, government buildings usually were underfunded and old. It was a humble profession to work at the government town hall. *But this? This is incredible!*

There were holographic people giving announcements on pedestals scattered throughout the floor and a projected, ginormous sea turtle swimming across the walls upward in a spiral. There were floating banners with the words flickering across: *Memory fades, but Reminserum is forever.* They were standing on the ground floor in the center, like the eye of a hurricane, and looking up, they could see straight through to the sky and feel the sun's warm rays.

"Is the top just open?" Sage gasped at the magnitude of the building.

"Yup. We're standing in the center courtyard. They call it the Main Atrium. The top of this is open with no roof. Surrounding the center courtyard are the offices and walkways. It's designed this way so every room has access to fresh air. The government, top urban architects, and psychologists found that this layout helps with stress-relief, encourages natural collaboration, and strengthens a culture of togetherness and harmony." Lewis beamed but then quickly fell serious. "I mean, I know we've learned a lot about the GMA and the Prime Minister that are unsavory. But they take care of many people and work hard to encourage community."

"They don't take care of *everyone,* though..." Sage humphed.

"You're right. But that's easy for you to say as someone who's not from here," Lewis retorted with a tinge of sourness. At hearing that uncharacteristic emotion from Lewis, Mel realized this whole situation must have flipped his world and everything he knew upside down. He'd been logical and open, but that didn't mean he wasn't struggling with the lies that his society may be built upon.

"Lewis, we don't mean to judge," Mel started.

"It's okay. I know you don't mean to. I just got a bit frustrated." He heaved a big sigh.

"What happens if it rains then? Would everyone just get wet?" Sage had already moved on.

"There's a glass screen that slides out when it rains," Lewis answered.

"So..." Marcus interrupted. Mel had forgotten he was right next to them. "You all going to tune me into what's going on?" he asked expectantly.

"I'll explain later, Marcus, so no questions for now," Lewis responded. Mel realized their comments must have seemed strange to him as he didn't know they came from another world. For all he knew, they were just other kids from around here.

To her surprise, Marcus nodded and added no further questions.

Other than the swimming projection of the sea turtle and floating banners, there was also a large waterfall feature that started midair halfway up the building, crashed onto rounded stones that jutted out of the floor, and trickled into a stream along the glossy courtyard floor before seamlessly disappearing underneath. Other than the office workers strolling purposefully, a few smiling enforcers were standing around.

"What's the difference between the enforcers with the silver lining and those with gold lining on their uniforms?" Sage asked as she observed a few.

Marcus looked at them with curiosity. "You don't know that? The enforcers with silver embroidery are our community enforcers. These are the ones we see all the time. You'll see there are more of them. Occasionally, you'll see one with gold lining on their uniforms. Those enforcers are usually here at MAGMA headquarters because they're the Prime Minister's special forces. They rank higher than the other enforcers. It's a hard job and noble career."

Mel remembered the enforcers who came looking for them and took Mrs. Trisham had the gold lining. *That's how Mrs. Trisham knew they were deployed by the Prime Minister.*

"This is the Main Atrium," the tour guide announced to the class. "Most MAGMA buildings are more traditional, but headquarters is the pinnacle of development and technology, so the Prime Minister wanted the design of the building to reflect such. Today, we'll take you through some of our labs and offices in case any of you want to work at MAGMA when you're grown up. We'll also take you through a Memory Room and the Prime Minister's office." There were a few excited whispers.

"We can see where he sits and works!"

"Maybe I'll see my dad here when he's working!"

"Everyone here looks so smart!"

The chaperones hushed the chatter. The tour guide continued. "We'll end the tour with a rooftop picnic. Courtesy of our Prime Minister."

The class broke out in excited exclamations. A few office workers walked past, looked at them, and smiled kindly.

They received an escort toward the first location: a proper Memory Room. Mel was quite curious as the only one she'd seen was Romilda's submarine rendition.

A few other classmates had looked at Mel and Sage strangely, but with Lewis and Marcus acting like it was normal, they just shrugged it off. Not their problem.

The tour guide took them downstairs on a large freight elevator. *So, the Memory Rooms are all held underground,* Mel noted.

The elevator gently dinged, and the doors slid open, but instead of stopping at the extent of the opening, the walls of the elevator continued sliding back as the doors did until both ends met behind them, melting into nothingness at the seam. They were now standing at the center of a large, softly lit, circular room, with multiple doors, equidistant from one another, along the circumference of the room. There were designated numbers above the doors, almost like a theater. Mel's mind finally caught up to her observation. *Hold on... we didn't even step outside of the elevator.*

Sage tugged at Mel's sleeve. "Weren't we in an elevator? And now we're in a room?" Mel only had time to respond with a shrug before the tour guide continued.

"This way." Their steps echoed on the floor as the group walked toward the door marked with an illuminated *nine* above it.

When they entered, they found themselves in another cylindrical room, but the walls were made of curved screens with gray smoke billowing across. Following the screens upward, Mel couldn't tell where the ceiling started and the wall ended. *This is much larger than the Memory Room on Romilda's submarine.*

The tour guide cleared his throat. "Adults will take Reminserum before entering. The room then scans their biodata to link up. We have technicians in the back adjusting the display and helping bring the requested memory to the screens. As you see, it's surround sound and fully immersive for people to best experience their memories again. Once the memory starts, the adult may pause at any time, fast-forward, rewind, or zoom into any detail. Truly trailblazing technology to help our community remember. As you all know, memory fades, but Reminserum is forever."

Mel's scalp tingled in alarm at hearing the phrase on the yellow posters repeated.

Most students were familiar with Memory Rooms, so a few yawned conspicuously. The tour guide noticed and very soon filed everyone back out. Mel, though, was quite impressed by the largeness of it and how it worked and wished the tour guide had gone into more details.

"Next up is the Prime Minister's office!" the tour guide announced, which reinvigorated many students' spirits as the previous silence was broken by excited squeals.

This is it. Sage, Mel, and Lewis exchanged glances and nodded at each other.

"Remember," Lewis put his arms around them again and pulled them into a huddle, "when we spot the device, Sage will create a distraction outside. There should be a fire alarm to pull outside the office near the restrooms. I'll make a run for the shelf that the device is on, grab it, and stuff it into my backpack. Mel, you keep watch. Use the walkie-talkies to communicate to Sage when I've grabbed the item, so she knows we're good to go."

"Got it," Mel said. "But is it okay that Marcus just heard everything?" She pointed at Marcus, who had been standing next to them this whole time.

"Are you kidding me?" Marcus looked at them with incredulity, "You can't do this and not let me be a part of it. I don't know what's going on, but grabbing something from the oh-so-beloved Prime Minister's office? I'm in!" Marcus volunteered himself. Mel and Sage looked at Lewis with raised brows.

"Some of us *do* think the love for Prime Minister Gio is kind of ridiculous. And I trust Marcus. He can help Sage." He nodded approvingly. Mel wasn't so sure but saw they'd decided.

They slowly drifted apart as the class headed to the office: Marcus with Sage and Mel with Lewis. Mel wasn't very happy to separate from Sage, but Sage looked ecstatic to be with Marcus.

Mel assumed they were getting closer as they entered official-looking hallways with plush blue carpet. Marcus and Sage slipped away from the group to get to the restrooms right before the tour guide dramatically pushed open two seven-foot-tall French doors to reveal a smartly decorated office. The class was now inside the Prime Minister's office.

It was also a circular room, with a desk at the far side from the entrance. If the Prime Minister were sitting there, he'd be facing them. Before his desk was a sitting area with a coffee table and couches. The left and right sides of the room were not walls but horizontally split, with the top half of the wall as curved tanks and the bottom half as bookshelves. The tanks were aquascaped with stones, plants, and coral. The left tank had white sand with various colorful fish flitting about, whereas the right tank had black sand with five large Arowana fish slowly making rounds. *Each of those must be at least three feet long!* Mel never thought a fish could look intimidating, but these fish with dragon-like scales seemed constantly tensed to attack each other, slowly biding their time.

Behind the Prime Minister's desk were two shelves full of books, plaques, medals, and assorted items.

One of them looked familiar. Mel looked to Lewis, and he indicated that he saw it too. *I can't believe it. Grandpa's device is here! Just as Lewis saw it in the magazine!* Mel took the walkie-talkie out of her pocket and pressed the button to whisper through. "We found it!" After a moment, there was a disturbance outside the office. Marcus was yelling something, followed by the ringing of the fire alarm.

Everyone's attention turned away from the office toward the commotion. The enforcers standing at the doorway ran out to control the situation. *Now's the moment!* Lewis had already sprinted to the desk across the room, reached up, and grabbed the device. However, it was heavier than he'd imagined, and he immediately had to set the device onto the floor first to wrestle it into his backpack. There was still yelling occurring outside when Sage's voice came through the walkie-talkie.

"Did he get it? Are we good?"

"No, not yet! Keep going! I think he's having trouble putting it away," Mel frantically updated her.

"But I don't know how long Marcus can distract them!" Sage's voice sounded unsure.

"Young man, get back here!" someone hollered outside. *Are they chasing Marcus?* Mel checked on Lewis and saw him still struggling. She rushed over to help.

"It's much heavier than it looks," Lewis grunted.

"I'll open the backpack," Mel quickly suggested. "You take the device with both hands to lift and place it in." Lewis did as instructed; he took the device and stood to lift it high enough to place it into the backpack. Mel positioned the bag below it so he could place it in easily.

"What are you two doing there?" An enforcer was standing at the doorway of the empty office. An enforcer with gold lining.

CHAPTER 19

Lewis had just carefully placed the device into the backpack that Mel held open, but it was too late. A special forces enforcer saw them and started to stalk toward them.

"You two. What did you just take?" she demanded.

"I... uh... dropped something," Lewis mustered but it sounded like quite the feeble excuse to Mel when clearly, the enforcer saw them steal the device.

"Lewis!" she desperately whispered to him from the corner of her mouth.

"I know!" He zipped up the backpack and slung it around his shoulders. "We need to split. They're going to want the device, so they'll come after me first if I'm holding the backpack."

"What!" *This wasn't part of the plan.* Mel was about to object, but the enforcer was upon them already, and Lewis had straightened up.

"You won't get it!" he yelled to the enforcer as he spun around her and raced toward the door.

"Get back here!" the special enforcer roared as she ran after him.

This is my chance! Mel stood up, her quickening heart-beat screaming inside her to run. *It sounded like the enforcers were only chasing Marcus earlier. I'll first meet up with Sage then.* Mel pressed the button to speak into the walkie-talkie.

"Sage, you there?" No answer, but there was no time to wait. *Lewis is buying me time by distracting the enforcer. I need to get out of here for now.* She headed toward the doorway as well, but suddenly, the hairs on the back of her neck stood, sending shivers down her spine as she felt a presence behind her.

While watching Lewis evade the enforcer plus trying to contact Sage, Mel hadn't noticed the hidden door behind the bookcases had soundlessly slid open, and the person who exited was right behind her. She swiveled to face him in alarm but felt a sudden *thwack* at the back of her head, and all went black.

***

Mel's eyes were closed, but she could feel her hands and her body. It felt like she was floating, but she could sense her body was on a firm surface. She tried to lift her arms, but they felt heavy and wouldn't budge. There was gray smoke coming into her sight, yet she knew her eyes were closed. It was the same sensation Mel sometimes got when she tried to wake up from a dream.

I can't get up. I can't wake up!

Then, the smoke dissipated almost as quickly as it had appeared. She tried wriggling her fingers and found she could move them again. She wriggled her toes. *It works.* She slowly, finally opened her eyes.

The sight of her desk and shelves of books came to view. She popped up and surveyed her surroundings. She was in her own bed, at home. The wind blew through the small, open sliver of a window next to her. There was her bulletin board with notes, cards from friends, and pictures of her favorite shelter dogs.

"Mel, Sage! Wake up and get down for breakfast!" her mom's voice called from the kitchen downstairs.

I'm back home? But I thought... Mel thought she was somewhere else before but couldn't quite place it.

Her door swung open, interrupting her thoughts.

"Are you coming or not? Mom will get angry if we take too long," Sage bossily said as she stood at the doorway.

Sage! Thank goodness she's here. Mel felt relief flood through her, but she wasn't sure why. She'd seen Sage just last night at home, of course. She saw her every day. It puzzled her more.

"Mel! Sage!" their mom called impatiently.

Mel shook off her thoughts. *I need to dress! Mom's calling us for breakfast.*

"You go down first, Sage. I'll be there in a moment!" she instructed her. *Having one of them going down first would help assuage Mom.*

"All right." Sage trudged off. *Probably waiting for a show if Mom gets angry at me.* Mel rolled her eyes. She hastily slipped her pajamas off, squeezed through a training bra, and put on some denim shorts and a sweatshirt.

"I'm coming," she yelled into the nether of the house as she hopped on one foot, putting on socks. She grabbed a hair tie on the way out of her room, and as she headed toward the stairs, something shot out of the hallway closet and seized her wrist, causing her to yelp.

"Shhh. It's me," Sage peeped from the closet.

"Why'd you scare me?" Mel angrily yanked her hand back and rubbed it tenderly. "What're you doing in there?"

At that moment, Sage's voice shouted at her from the kitchen to hurry up.

"What?" *Why am I hearing Sage from downstairs too?* Mel looked at the Sage inside the closet next to her.

"That's not me, Mel. Don't go," this Sage pleaded. Mel felt her heart starting to race and her ears starting to ring, but then suddenly shut the closet door in her face.

"Not today, Satan!" she announced to herself and slapped herself with both hands three times. She slowly opened the closet again, but Sage was no longer there. Mel sighed in relief and ran downstairs.

Mom and Sage were already sitting at the table, and Dad was at the stove whipping up the last dish of stir-fried tomatoes and eggs.

"Girls, you can't keep us waiting. What took you so long, Mel?" Dad asked as he brought the last piping dish over.

"Sorry, I know. I overslept today," Mel said morosely.

"All right. You were still making the last dish, hun," Mom said to their dad. "We're all here now!"

Everyone had a steaming bowl of rice in front of them. Breakfast was the stir-fried tomatoes and eggs, some pickled radishes, fermented tofu, and slices of bamboo shoots soaked in chili oil. Mom and Dad asked about their homework. But something tugged at the recesses of Mel's mind. She eyed Sage suspiciously. *Sage would usually be annoyed she had already served the rice for everyone by herself. Why hasn't she complained about me being late yet?*

After breakfast, Mel volunteered to put up the dishes and wash them.

Mom entered the kitchen. "Set the dishes aside for now. You should help me make something so you can learn how to make it yourself when you go to college."

"Mom, there will probably be a cafeteria on campus. And we still have so many years!"

"What if it's your favorite dish?" Her mom turned to her with one brow raised and a slight smile.

"We're having Pearl Meatballs today?" *That deliciously juicy meatball in a soft coat of glutinous rice to create the most divine mouthfeel?* Mel suddenly felt a bit more motivated to stay even after scrubbing away at dishes.

Mom had rinsed and soaked the glutinous rice and bamboo leaves last night. The next step today was to mix the meat and spices to ball up into meatballs. Mel's favorite part was rolling the meatballs through the tray of rice to coat.

Mel's mom had set the mise en place on the counter, including ingredients that go into the meat to create that savory filling. Chopped ginger, scallion, mushrooms, garlic, salt, bowls of rice wine, and sesame oil. "Mix each of those into the meat bowl one by one. Not all at once like Sage did last time," Mel's mom directed.

In her excitement to learn, Mel had forgotten her earlier trepidation about the Sage in the closet until just now.

As she mixed the meat filling, the spoon created squelching noises as it smushed through the mix. The kitchen was a combination of these sounds, interspersed with pauses of adding ingredients, Mom checking the mixture, and Mom rustling about preparing the steamer. Mel's hands left wet sweat stains on the wooden spoon, and she was starting to feel warm, but it wasn't from mixing. It was an uncanny feeling. *I keep feeling I'm forgetting something. What did I forget? Did I forget to go volunteering?*

Mel paused her mixing, and the kitchen fell into an uncharacteristic stillness. *I did... I missed volunteering at the shelter. But why?*

The stillness reminded Mel that her mom never cooked in silence. She was usually humming to herself, watching a show in the background, or on the phone with another auntie to chat about someone's oh-so-accomplished child.

Something didn't line up.

"Hey, Mom?" Mel started. "Do you remember why I missed volunteering on Tuesday?"

Mom looked at her vacantly. "You went."

What is she talking about? Mel was positive she missed it.

"No, I don't think I did. Dad got upset at me, right? At the dinner table. For missing it?"

"Hmm, I'm not sure." Her mom started lining the steamer with paper. "Actually, I think he did. Maybe you missed it for an after-school club? Or... you were with Sage, right?"

Mel raised her brows. *It's not only Sage—Mom's acting suspiciously too. It's almost as if... she's searching for an answer to see which one I would say is right...*

At the ring of the doorbell, Mel headed to the doorway to see Beck, her best friend's, face plastered to the hazy windows at the door.

"Hey, Mel!" Beck greeted her warmly.

"What're you doing here?" Although Mel was happy to see her friend, she was confused why Beck had dropped by unheeded.

"You invited me over!" She stepped in and took off her shoes in the foyer. "Hey, Mrs. Yu!"

Mel looked at the calendar hanging on their wall and saw that it was the weekend. She only recalled inviting Beck for Wednesday.

Wait. What happened on Wednesday, Thursday, and Friday? She drew a blank on what she did those days. But then again, with school and volunteering, it wasn't uncommon for her to not remember details because it was so routine.

"Well, now that Becca is here, you guys can go off. I'll take care of the rest in the kitchen." Her mom had entered the foyer, wiping her hands on a towel.

"Thanks, Mrs. Yu!" Beck called. "By the way, I have some snacks that my mom wanted me to share." She brought out a large paper bag from behind her that was filled to the brim.

"That's very nice of your parents, Becca. Mel," Mom faced her, "help Becca put away the snacks she brought."

"Yeah, sure." Mel headed into the kitchen with Beck following.

Beck poured the contents of the paper bag onto the counter to reveal a sack of oranges and several bags of purple crescent-shaped chips.

Purple chips? I've never seen that before.

"What are these?" Mel asked, pointing to the crinkly bags. Beck looked at her with a mixture of surprise and... *worry?*

"What do you mean? They're chips."

"I can see that. I just mean, what flavor and where are they from? I've never seen them before."

"Oh, really?" Becca's pitch raised slightly. "These are pretty standard. I'm sure you've seen them in vending machines before." She started neatly stacking the chips into the pantry.

That triggered a memory on the tip of Mel's tongue. Now that Beck mentioned it, Mel did remember seeing them in a vending machine somewhere. *But it was a very specific place. Where have I seen it?*

"I know it's the weekend, but maybe we can work on our group history project today?" Beck suggested.

Mel was still thinking about where she'd seen those chips. "Oh, sure. On the Bronze Age, yeah?"

"What? You study the Bronze Age?" Beck guffawed before slapping a hand to her mouth.

Mel eyed her questioningly. Alarms were suddenly ringing in her head at Beck's reaction. *Someone else was surprised about the Bronze Age. Who was it...?*

Beck nervously opened a bag of purple chips to eat to fill the silence, and that's when it hit Mel.

Seeing the purple chips again on top of the surprise at their curriculum including the Bronze Age... *Hold on. Those chips are not from here. They were in a vending machine, yes. But it was that one old machine that took me to that other world. The world where Lewis's mom was shocked that we were learning about the Bronze Age instead of their Coral Age!*

It all came flooding back as if she opened a dam. *I was with Sage! We stumbled upon the Second Layer that Grandpa is from. Romilda! The government memory control! Lewis!*

She narrowed her eyes at Becca. "Becca, you're acting a bit weird."

"What?" she said blankly.

"Becca's fine, dear." Her mom had entered the kitchen again. Mel also eyed her mom.

"Actually, Mom, you've been strange, too." She looked at the chips Becca was holding. "In fact, those chips don't belong in this layer."

Both her mother and Becca stared at her, disturbingly silent.

"And if you're both pretending the chips are normal and that nothing happened that day I actually fell into the Second Layer with Sage, then..." Her eyes widened. The last thing she remembered was being in the Prime Minister's office. Lewis was running, and then... someone knocked her out. And she woke up here in a very strange place with strange people posing to be her friend and family.

I was in the Prime Minister's office. Is this weird world his doing?

"Then what?" the person who looked like her mother asked unblinkingly.

"This isn't real." Mel breathed deeply. "Your first mistake was showing me these chips that belong in your world, not mine," Mel explained out loud. "I'm stuck somewhere and don't know where, but I'm not home. And I remember everything that has happened. I know about you, Prime Minister." She found more strength as she spoke.

A pregnant silence hung in the air before the person who claimed to be Becca said, "What *are* you talking about, Mel. Are you frying your brains on the computer?" But Mel could not shake the inhuman stares they gave her and the purple chips right there, in addition to the oppressing air she'd felt ever since waking up.

"No, you don't need to pretend. Let me out now."

They stared.

"Let me out now!" Mel said more forcefully. She noticed microcracks forming along the kitchen walls and backsplash with gray smoke seeping through. *Gray smoke! Like… in the Memory Room screens!*

"You put me in a memory. You're making a memory? I don't know exactly what's going on, but you're messing with my head somehow, and it will not work because I know what's real. I *know* what's mine!"

"You don't know what you're talking about, darling," the fake mom said emotionlessly.

"Let me out *now*!" Mel demanded emphatically as the cracks deepened and spread to the flooring.

It was mental. She had to fight mentally.

"You will *not* erase my memories and make me forget like you do to your people. I *know* what's mine. If you don't let me out, I will *push* you out of my head. You get out of here *now*." She gradually raised her voice into a yell.

The cracks on the floor widened and sections were disintegrating. But the mom and Becca puppets weren't surprised at all as they stood still.

"*Get out!*" Mel roared, and suddenly the ground completely crumbled, and her stomach lurched as she fell through.

CHAPTER 20

Mel jerked awake from falling and found herself on a hospital bed in the middle of a massive, dark Memory Room. She sat up and looked around.

"So," a voice boomed. "You figured me out." A figure walked out from the shadows. A handsome face showed when the light hit him, and it was Prime Minister Gio in the flesh! He gestured to someone beyond the screen to stop, and all the lights turned on.

Mel jumped off the bed, ready to run.

"You have nowhere to go, Mel. That's why I found no reason to tie you down or lock you up either." He sounded bored.

"Where am I? Were you inside my head?"

He laughed deeply and slowly clapped. "Bravo, Mel, for figuring it out. Yes, I was. Imagine my surprise when I found you in my office as I came back through from my hidden door." He had started to circle Mel leisurely. "Wow, someone from the First Layer. When we first got a notification someone was using the machines, I thought it was a false alarm. There's no way someone could be using the vending portals. I'd gotten rid of the Envoy program, ensured everyone was taken care of, collected all tokens and materials for the program, and slowly wiped all memory of it over the decades by making sure no one recalled it. There was no way." He seemed to be talking to himself now.

"But when the second notification came for the usage of a Mastodon token specifically, I got concerned. Was a Mastodon member still around and remembering?" He scoffed and paused. "We pinpointed a general area of usage, and I sent all my enforcers as soon as I could to scour the whole area." He lifted his gaze to Mel. "My people were just about to miss you. Dr. Leo-Trisham's house of all places? She's one of my most trusted scientists!" The prime minister chuckled to himself. "Luckily, her daughter saw right through everything and notified us as my people were about to leave. Who knew you'd be children! You have no idea what you're doing." He giggled.

His joy angered her. They'd gone through so much. Her grandfather had fought for a cause against this very man. Enforcers had arrested Lewis's mom. Romilda had been hiding for decades. And he laughed at them?

"I know what you're up to!" Mel countered. "We know! You've been the same man all these years, pretending to pass down the prime minister position, but it's you! You give the community food and help them, but you just use all that to cover up the fact that you're basically erasing memories!"

His joyful face immediately darkened. "Oh? Seeing as you're from the First Layer, and yet you're saying all this, you did indeed receive help to know this much. Tell me. Who helped you?"

At that, Mel realized perhaps they hadn't caught Romilda, or they didn't know who she was. Prime Minister Gio spoke again.

"Let me first enlighten you, dear Mel. Our people are not blessed like yours to have control over our own memory recall. I help the people. I aid them in remembering with Reminserum. It's free of cost. I provide food and services to everyone. These are all things our people never have to worry about. On top of that, it revolutionized our society when we discovered this solution—with perfect memory archives and each citizen as a living surveillance camera, our crime rates exponentially decreased to close to zilch." He inhaled deeply with a look of euphoria.

"So what if you do all that? You're watching everyone's memories, and you don't let them remember things you don't want! You're erasing memories and history!"

"Hush, young one. I've seen numerous decades of strife, and the times have never been more peaceful than now. International conflict? Well, let's just not recall that public gaff or sentiment to hold a grudge. Emotional worries or anger at someone? Let's just not recall those moments they're thinking of. Everyone has a reason, memory, or experience for why they feel a certain way or why they prescribe to a cause or platform. Forget those, and the polarization and conflicts won't arise." Prime Minister Gio twirled lightly on his feet. "Forgetting is the first step to forgiveness for a kinder world. For the good of our society."

His words mortified Mel. *He isn't just erasing memories and history. He's erasing personalities! People's reason for being themselves!*

"Just because people have different thoughts and argue about them doesn't mean you need to step in and take away their memories. That's between them!"

He chuckled. "Have you not seen this place?" He gestured to the entire room. "Have you not seen this world I built? It took me generations, but I made it. My people are happy."

Mel thought for a moment. "Don't you want them happy on their own? Conflicts and arguments aren't all bad. We learn from it." She remembered her mom always said this.

He waved her off like any adult waves off children. "You'll never understand, and my conversation with you on this is pointless. Back to who helped you..." He crossed his arms pensively. "Could it be possible that Dr. Leo-Trisham helped you? Her husband was previously a problem, what a pity, and she doesn't know of that. I thought she got caught up in this because of her son, but perhaps..."

"No! She didn't know about us at all. We didn't tell her anything," Mel frantically blurted. She didn't want Lewis's family getting into more trouble than needed.

"Oh? We? So, her son *did* know about you. We'll have to look into that. We'll probably have to monitor him until he's eighteen. Naturally, the problem will take care of itself after that," the Prime Minister mumbled to himself.

He didn't mention Sage... perhaps he doesn't have her? Mel tried to make sure her face didn't reveal anything as she tried to figure it out.

"Did you... see anything else in my memories?" *Does he know Sage is in the building, too?*

"Oh, Mel. It's not an exact science. I can't just go into your head and find things like a file. It depends on the memory that you are recalling. You happened to be thinking about home, so that's the one I could go in and play with. This is a new feature we're beta-testing called Memory Warping. I was trying to see if I could get you to think all this," he waved around, "was a dream. If I can successfully do so, then my job is done, and we can drop you right back into the First Layer. But I made a few mistakes, and you saw right through it." He looked behind him into the darkness and yelled, "You're noting down the results, right? We can't repeat this error."

Mel breathed a sigh of relief that he didn't mention Sage, but now she had to buy time as she thought about her next course of action. "So, you can't read all memories, but you can control memories?"

"I don't control their memories. I restrict it. People need Reminserum and come to MAGMA to help them recall what they want to recall. It goes through our systems first, and if it's something on our blacklisted topics, we divert it to an associated memory. Slightly complicated but relatively simple once we built the systems and algorithms. This was the first time I tried Memory Warping, though. It wasn't successful, but we collected some precious data. If it could work on someone from the First Layer with no memory issues as we do here, it would most definitely work for anyone in the Second Layer." He nodded to someone behind the screens again.

"Now, during that little session we had earlier, you had memories of your sister. Sage, was it?"

Mel gulped. *So, he does know about Sage!*

"We couldn't see much, but," he put a hand to an earpiece Mel only now saw and seemed to listen for a moment, "it seems she's quite important to you. Would she also be here, Mel?" He cocked his head.

"No," Mel said, attempting to be calm. "I was just thinking of my sister at home. I came here on my own and then met Lewis."

The Prime Minister nodded, ordering through his earpiece, "Search the building just in case." Mel's heart dropped. Did she just indicate to them that Sage was around when they didn't know before? But she also wanted to know the truth.

"So, you admit to everything? The memory restrictions? Being in power all this time? How is that possible for decades? How do you still look... young?"

He laughed. "You know, the more I tell you, the less likely you'll be going home, right? So be it. My family is a family of alchemy scientists who've been chasing the elixir of youth."

Mel's mouth was agape. *What Captain Pilazzo said is true?*

"A legend—I know. But my family searched for generations. When we finally found it, I was just a young boy then, but they let me take it as an experiment. They locked me up. Studied my cells to see if this was possible to dilute as a vaccine of sorts for the general public. Or to sell to the highest bidder—I don't know. They prodded me. They starved me—anything to run testing scenarios. Fortunately, my grandmother took pity on me, and perhaps she had compounded guilt. But near the end of her life, she petitioned to free me. They'd tried the elixir on a few other subjects, such as my cousins, but they all died or retained a child's body. It was a failure. I was the only one who was fine, and they were keen to hold on.

But it had been several years, and out of respect for my grandmother, I suppose they decided to close the project. I then tried to live normally and worked my way up politically, and when I finally made prime minister, I had great pride in it. The boy who'd been locked up for half his life as an experiment was now in the highest seat of power. People looked up to me. I then noticed my body stopped aging in my forties as a side-effect of the elixir. I had to dye my hair gray. Use makeup for artificial wrinkles. Through this, I realized I had the opportunity to do something only I could do for everyone. I could create the perfect place. The perfect society. Where everyone's fed, not fearful of the government, and happy. Additionally, I can prevent the remembrance of bad things so we aren't burdened by our ugly pasts or unneeded misunderstandings. That's when we started creating the algorithm of blacklisted topics."

"But why?" Mel was appalled at how his family treated him but still couldn't understand why he was doing this.

"I want to create a place where there's no fear and where everyone of value belongs."

"What about the people in those neighborhoods that you restrict access to? And the blinded Envoys?

"You know about that? Those people bring no value. There's no reason to let them remember things as long as I'm feeding them. They can just sit at home or do whatever job they do. But their memories are not valuable to the good of this society I'm building. And the blinded Envoys? They're remnants of an old system. I could not have people knowing and remembering that another world existed."

"Why does that matter? Why don't you want them to know about another world?"

"That's because the people in your layer, Mel, have full access to their own memories. My people don't, so they need me. I look after them. They don't need to know about what they don't have. They'll be grateful for what I offer. If they knew, it would jeopardize everything I've created."

"You can't do that! You can't just withhold knowledge because you're worried about how people will react! We all have bad memories, but so what? My mom's always said every bad experience is a learning experience. You're not letting your own people grow!"

"They don't need to be concerned with that if I'm here to help them. And it's too late. I'm already successful at it, and you can't do anything about it because no one else knows." He smiled blissfully at Mel's despair that she could likely be the last and only person to know everything.

Suddenly, multiple doors flew open from around the circular room of screens, and enforcers flowed in. The gold-embroidered ones flocked to the Prime Minister, while the silver-embroidered ones stood before them in fighting stances. It was a face-off.

"What are you all doing here? I told you to search the building for another girl," he said impatiently to them.

One of the silver enforcers stepped forward. It was Enforcer Jovanna! Mel's heart lifted at seeing a familiar face. "Sir, with all due respect, we're here for you. You're under arrest."

"Excuse me?" Prime Minister Gio took an offended tone. "I demand you to stand down. If you refuse, I have the special enforcers here who rank higher. Remember your place."

"I do, sir," Enforcer Jovanna responded. "It's my duty to ensure the safety of our citizens, and from what we heard, you've been abusing your power and our trust in you. You are a danger to our people, so it's my mandate to hold you accountable."

The Prime Minister frenetically combed the room with his eyes. "I'm a danger and threat to our people? I only do the most for you all!"

"Sir, let's not escalate this. We understand your enforcers rank higher, but that's just because they're your private force. We all went through the same training." He pressed a remote button in his hand, and it elongated from both ends into a vibrating staff. The other silver-embroidered enforcers produced their glowing ropes that almost seemed to hiss. "We're not afraid to neutralize your men and women."

"They heard everything. The ruse is over." Romilda stepped up, and a little head popped out from behind her.

"Sage!" Mel rushed to embrace her, but Prime Minister Gio lunged for Mel at that moment. She felt his nails graze her back, but one of the silver enforcers quickly maneuvered forward and blocked him.

"You're okay, Sage!"

Before she could ask more, Enforcer Jovanna presented Mrs. Trisham's tape recorder. "This young lady named Sage brought this recording to us with concerning claims of your wrongdoings. Fortunately, we had Dr. Leo-Trisham in our holdings, so we brought her and Romilda out, took them to a Memory Room to get to the bottom of it, and ensured our Memory Room engineers disabled the blacklisted topics for unfiltered recall. Once we saw the memories that corroborated with the recording, there was no denying what you've done, Prime Minister."

The usually handsome face of the Prime Minister contorted in disbelief as Jovanna continued. "You're under arrest, sir. We will be conducting an investigation into this to determine the extent of your plans and who else may be involved."

His men surged forward with precision, disarmed the gold enforcers, and immediately tossed the glowing ropes around the Prime Minister's hands.

"You can't do this to me! This is a coup! Insurgency!" the Prime Minister spat.

"Bring that to court then," Enforcer Jovanna responded calmly, and they carried the Prime Minister away.

CHAPTER 21

Mel looked at Sage as the silver enforcers led the gold ones and the Prime Minister away.

"What happened, Sage? I thought you'd get caught!"

"I'm so happy to see you!" Sage gave her another squeeze before explaining. "Marcus had helped set off the alarm when you and Lewis were in the Prime Minister's office. I was keeping watch, but then an enforcer took Marcus. I was going to warn you, but it was too late. Then, when I saw an enforcer chasing Lewis, I thought I could get to you, but when I got to the door, I saw this man knock you out! I flipped out and didn't enter the room. But I saw him take you through some hidden door in the back. It's a good thing I had this blazer uniform Lewis found so I could blend in with the school. But I didn't know what to do."

"I happened to have been speaking to my superior when I saw her." Enforcer Jovanna had come back. "I recognized her from the park that day with Lewis and just saw that gold-embroidered enforcer chase Lewis down, so I wanted to ask her about it."

"And since Lewis said such good things about him, I knew he had to be a good person and asked him for help. I had to do something!"

"Yes, she pulled me to an emptier hallway and told me everything. I, naturally, didn't believe her at first. I thought she was pulling some prank. Kids can be brutal these days." He gave a tired sigh.

"But then I remembered I had Mrs. Trisham's recording!" Sage excitedly recounted.

"When she took that out and played it, I was still dubious as someone could have doctored it, but I also knew that Dr. Leo-Trisham was in our custody." He scratched his head as he added, "I was asking my superior about it earlier since she's a friend."

He then handed the two of them some granola bars from his pockets. "Sorry, this is the only thing I have right now, but I thought you may be hungry." Mel gratefully took it, and he continued.

"So, against protocol, I released Dr. Leo-Trisham so I could ask about the recording. Sage had also told me about Romilda, so imagine my surprise when I saw her name on the holdings list as well. I got her out too and brought them to a Memory Room. Fortunately, after we finished, we heard your voice, Mel."

"You heard me? How?"

"As you were yelling the heck out of the Prime Minister!" Sage announced proudly. "We were in a nearby Memory Room."

Enforcer Jovanna nodded. "We got very lucky. Needless to say, I was shocked to hear of the Prime Minister's monopoly on our memories and our leadership. It's against everything they tell us about the government and confirmed everything Sage said. I made a quick judgment call and immediately mobilized my team to get to you and Gio Bellows."

"Where are Mrs. Trisham and Lewis?" Mel asked.

She suddenly felt someone wrap their arms around her warmly from behind. She turned her head to see. "Lewis!"

Enforcer Jovanna laughed. "We interrogated one of the Prime Minister's special enforcers for Lewis's location. When he wouldn't spill, it was easy enough to extract the information in a Memory Room with some memory prompting to figure out where they locked him and his friend up."

"Yeah! Enforcer Jovanna's people came and saved us! And my mom's speaking with a few other enforcers outside," Lewis added.

Mel felt relief wash through her body.

"What's going to happen to him?" Sage asked about the Prime Minister.

"We'll be doing some investigations. But what we saw in the Memory Room plus the recording constitute incriminating evidence of very serious offenses to our community. But also, he's well-loved by many. So, we have to be careful about how we approach this. Don't you worry about this, though. It's my job." He grinned from ear to ear.

"I believe I can help with that." Romilda had come back after helping the silver enforcers handle the gold enforcers.

"Romilda!" Mel, Lewis, and Sage surged forward to hug her. "What happened to you on the cliffs?"

Her eyes sparkled into a smile. "Happy to see you all doing okay, too, kids. There were too many of them on the cliffs, and at my old age," she chuckled, "I knew I couldn't hold them all off." She looked at Enforcer Jovanna.

"Allow me to formally introduce myself even though you've seen my memories. I'm one of the remaining members of the Mastodons, and we have extensive research on Gio Bellows. I can help you with your investigations and share what we have."

His eyes widened. "Incredible. So, the network is still alive? It's real."

"As real as it can be," Romilda agreed. "There should be a few more Mastodons in the GMA somewhere, too. I also knew your grandmother." She winked at him. "But first, I need to get these two ladies back home."

"As in, their world?" Enforcer Jovanna asked. "I can't have you doing that yet. I need to interview them."

"You'll have everything you need for your investigation with me, Enforcer. They haven't been home. They've been running and stuck in a strange world. I think they miss their family, right?" She looked at Mel and Sage.

"You can get us back?"

"Of course, I can," she responded as if they had just asked the most obvious question. "I'm an Envoy."

"And you'll come back?" Enforcer Jovanna inquired. "You won't mind if I send one of my enforcers with you?"

"As long as you're not locking me up or forcing me anywhere, that's fine," Romilda said. "Come on, girls, let's get you home."

"Um," Lewis said. "May I come too?"

They all looked at him.

"I'd like to say goodbye."

Romilda gave a soft smile. "That sounds like a good idea."

"Are you sure?" Enforcer Jovanna interrupted. "Your mom might get worried, Lewis. She's still helping us outside."

"It'll be fine," Romilda assured him. "Just tell her he's saying goodbye. I'll bring him back. And like you said, one of your enforcers will be with us."

Enforcer Jovanna thought about it before acquiescing. And so, the four of them headed out the building with an enforcer trailing a respectful distance behind them.

"Do we have to go to the park?" Sage asked Romilda.

"The park?"

"Yeah, the park with the vending machine. Or the bus stop," Mel added.

"Ah, I see you have used portals 5 and 17. We can utilize any vending machine here in the Second Layer. All of them are portals. You just have to know how to use them."

"Are you saying any common citizen could have been sucked into another world this entire time?" Lewis said, aghast.

Romilda convulsed with laughter. "The chances of that are slim. Everyone here belongs in the Second Layer. Even if we accidentally meet the right conditions, the portal would not just pull people in because they belong in this layer. Mel and Sage were able to accidentally get back home last time once they activated the machine because the First Layer was pulling them in since they belong there."

"But what about when we even got here in the first place?" Mel asked. "We don't belong in the Second Layer."

"Have you forgotten where your grandfather was from?"

Sage loudly gasped. "We're partially from the Second Layer because of Grandpa?"

"That's right. It's in your blood. That's the only reason I can think of the portal pulling you here."

They had reached a vending machine a few blocks from MAGMA headquarters. "Now, you have an activation code as well as a token to use to fully control where to go." Romilda selected multiple beverages by clicking on the keypad, but she didn't grab them as they dropped. Instead, she held her hand out.

"Mel, your token, please. Keep it around your neck though, so it stays with you as you travel."

Mel stepped forward with it. "I just put it in and twist it?"

"Yes. It registers the home location, which Howler already programmed to the one near your house in the First Layer. I checked. Typically, these vending portals have a three-foot radius to pull people when activated, but I inserted the additional code to only pull those with the key and those touching that person. So, Mel, you'll have to put the key in, and Sage, you need to make sure you're holding onto Mel."

Mel and Sage held hands and turned to Lewis and Romilda.

"Will we see you again?" Sage asked hopefully.

"Even though you have Second Layer blood, you don't belong here," Romilda explained softly. "With the Prime Minister arrested, things are about to get rocky around here. You both should stay away, especially since you're from another world. People could have mixed feelings about you being here, and they could turn on you if they believe in the Prime Minister. The GMA is potentially in a frail state now that it's lost its leader, and even if you helped divulge horrible things that Gio was doing, the current high members of the GMA would still be wary of you both. I wanted to get you both home as soon as we could—before more people found out. We'll straighten things out, but you likely won't see us for a while. That's why I'm not telling you the exact codes to use on the vending machines. And I put a lock on your grandfather's token."

"What?"

"Look at the key. There's a metallic dot on there. It's called a Restrictor, and it locks the Envoy from using the token other than the one trip. Only I can remove it. We used to use it if we had to suspend an Envoy."

"You can't do that to us!" Sage argued.

"I can and I will to keep Howler's grandchildren safe." She cupped their faces fondly. "Believe me when I say things will not be looking great here for a while."

Lewis finally spoke up. "I think Romilda is right. Tensions will start to mount. There may be public pressure to release the Prime Minister during the investigation. Then, who knows what he'll do if you're both still around?"

Mel thought about it, and that made sense. Sage, too, was silent at that. The thought of the Prime Minister getting his way was scary.

Lewis came forward and pulled the two of them into a hug. "I'll miss you both. And I won't forget you. Even when I turn eighteen." He pulled away and grinned.

"Are you done yet?" the enforcer who was instructed to follow them called from five feet away.

"Time to go." Romilda pushed them toward the machine.

Mel held Sage's hand tightly and inserted Grandpa's key. But before twisting it, she remembered something and turned back.

"What about the device? Grandpa's device we found at the Prime Minister's office?"

Romilda cracked a wry smile and opened her trench coat to reveal the device somehow hanging within it. "After I aided the enforcers in putting the Prime Minister's people away, I grabbed it. His men had returned it to the office after they caught Lewis. So, perhaps we'll be seeing more vending portals in the First Layer sometime soon."

At that, Mel twisted the key.

EPILOGUE

Mel meandered through the school library for the section on marine biology and animals.

It's been three months since Mel and Sage returned from the Second Layer. They'd gotten another earful from their parents for being unaccounted for that whole day, and yet no matter how much Dad chastised them and Mom threw disapproving looks, Mel and Sage both sneaked into their parents' room that night to sleep, much to their parents' surprise.

Nevertheless, Dad forbade them from wandering to the rice fields for a while. Even though Mel thought about the Second Layer often, she frankly wasn't too keen on going back soon. *It's much quieter here.*

She was enjoying flipping leisurely through illustrations of various sea life on the library floor and soaking in the sunlight that streamed in through the windows when out of the corner of her eyes, the tails of a trench coat flapped behind the books on the shelf in front of her.

She scrambled up and ran to the other side to look, only to find no one else there. A disappointment crept into her chest as she rationalized with herself. *I must be imagining things. There's no way Romilda would be here. I wonder how Lewis and everyone are doing...*

Mel returned and gathered a hefty five books to a table for perusing. She stacked her books neatly, plopped herself down, and picked up the first one on the Mariana Trench, the deepest ocean floor depression discovered so far. *That'll be a good one.*

As she opened the book, however, she heard a muffled beeping. Instinctively, she took out her phone but found it wasn't from that. Puzzled, she listened more carefully and realized it wasn't her phone's usual tone, and it was coming from her chest. *Could it be?*

Mel reached within her shirt and pulled out Grandpa's token. Now in the open, the token beeped with clarity. *It emits sounds? No one's mentioned they beep! What does this mean?* She looked around to ensure no one else was present before bringing the key closer to her face to examine it. That's when she noticed something was missing! The metallic Restrictor Romilda had installed on it was gone!

Does that mean...?

Mel hastily texted Sage before grabbing her book bag and dashing out. As she ran through the streets, she dialed her sister's number to call for extra measure.

"What does your text mean?" Sage picked up excitedly.

"Hurry and get here, Sage! They're calling for us!"

ACKNOWLEDGMENTS

Thank you to everyone who's been a part of my book journey. This would not have been possible without you and your passionate support, and it's been so warming to the soul to see everyone come from all walks of my life, all around the world, to support this.

I'd like to start by thanking my family—my sister and parents—for being my number one cheerleaders through this process.

A special thank you to Hailin for always being down to listen and bounce ideas and to Swetha for parrying thoughts with me to the wire.

Next, I'd like to thank my invested beta readers whose enthusiasm and feedback pushed me forward when it felt dark: Adiba C, Andy, Anisha, Danielle, Dixita, Hailin, Megha, Nritya, Swetha, and Vaishali & Peter.

I'd be remiss not to thank the incredible team at New Degree Press, including Eric Koester, Brian Bies, Melody Delgado Lorbeer, and Jessica Drake-Thomas, who not only led me through the process but also believed in me even during trying times. Thank you for making my longtime dream of sharing my brainchild with the world come true.

A massive thank you to this community of incredible people who believed in me so strongly they preordered their copies and helped promote the book before it even went to print:

Ace Motas	Ajay Subramanian
Alexander Morgan	Alexandra Gibner*
Alisa Quemado	Alisha Zou
Amber Liu*	Andreea L Panfiloiu
Andy Lau	Angela Guo
Angela Luo	Anisha Kolla
Anita Kapyur	Arjun Krishna
Ashley Buchanan	Ashley Espinoza
Ayush Narayan*	Benjamin Laun
Bethany Wong	Bo Kim
Carey Liu	Carolina Roberts
Cheng-Chuan Liu	Christina Tolkamp*
Cindy Lin	Corin Peterson
Dan Li	Danielle Rossi
Danni Vasquez	David Lam
David Sims	Dixita Viswanath
Eliza Posada	Emily Chang
Emily Gurvis	Eric Koester
Eric Lee	Erin O'Neill
Eshan Kejriwal	Esteban Pimentel
Eunju Pak*	Fatima Alvi
Gahbrielle Armardi*	Gurjit Singh*
Hailin Wang*	Hiren Patel
Jacqueline Nguyen	Jay Song
JC Kuo & Mae Kuo**	Jennifer Ding
Jennifer Tucker	Jesse Pegram
Jian Ming Dai*	John & Jenny Chen*

Jonathan Thomas
Joshua Buchholtz
Joshua White
Karen Hong
Kathleen Glass
Kathryn Kundrot
Katie Harvey
Kevin Shen Chang
Kristie Yit
Kuo T Huang
Leticia Trevino*
Lisa Auyeung
Lucy Xie
Manja Kovincic
Matthew Gates*
Meera Devarajan
Melissa D'Cruz
Nana Xu
Navneesh Pandher
Nimish Mittal

Olivia Hu and David Li
Rebecca Ho Van Dyke
Rohan Krishna
Ryan Liu
Sajeel Malik
Sean Dilliard
Sherice Lee
Sneha Joshi
Swetha Kotamraju
Tech Kuo
Tim Maxwell

Jordan Falk
Joshua Vuglar
Kai Sheng
Karen Qiang
Kathleen Lee
Kathy Truong
Kevin George*
Krishna Thiagarajan
Kristin Satterfield
Lavanya Rao
Linh-Tran Do
Louise Li*
Lyric Isabella Johnson
Margaret Lin
Meagan Thompson*
Megha Ramappan
Meng-Yu Wang
Natalia Majewska
Neha Pal
Nritya Kamath and
Kiran Pathakota
Poh Ko
Regan Wang
Ryan Chen*
Saikrishna Kalla
San-Pei Lee
Shelby D Kuhn
Sindhu Sathees
Sukejna Kovacevic
Tanvi Sharma
Teddy Schenkman
Timothy Lee

Tom Boughton
Vaishali Bhakta
Wen-Pen Liu and
Yang-Ching Liu*
Xiaochun Zhou
Yinjie Ji
Yoshimi Nakamura

Tommy Tang*
Vikram Murali
William Duong

Xiaoyi Li
Yoseph Maguire

* Extra donations or multiple copies purchased